Boosting
AI Autonomous
Cars

Practical Advances in
Artificial Intelligence and Machine Learning

Dr. Lance B. Eliot, MBA, PhD

Disclaimer: This book is presented solely for educational and entertainment purposes. The author and publisher are not offering it as legal, accounting, or other professional services advice. The author and publisher make no representations or warranties of any kind and assume no liabilities of any kind with respect to the accuracy or completeness of the contents and specifically disclaim any implied warranties of merchantability or fitness of use for a particular purpose. Neither the author nor the publisher shall be held liable or responsible to any person or entity with respect to any loss or incidental or consequential damages caused, or alleged to have been caused, directly or indirectly, by the information or programs contained herein. Every company is different and the advice and strategies contained herein may not be suitable for your situation.

DEDICATION

To my incredible daughter, Lauren, and my incredible son, Michael.

Forest fortuna adiuvat (from the Latin; good fortune favors the brave).

CONTENTS

Acknowledgments iii

Introduction 1

Chapters

1 Eliot Framework for AI Self-Driving Cars 15

2 Zero Knowledge Proofs and AI Self-Driving Cars 29

3 Active Shooter Response and AI Self-Driving Cars 61

4 Free Will and AI Self-Driving Cars 83

5 No Picture Yet of AI Self-Driving Cars 107

6 Boeing 737 Lessons and AI Self-Driving Cars 113

7 Preview Tesla FSD and AI Self-Driving Cars 121

8 LIDAR Industry and AI Self-Driving Cars 129

9 Uber IPO and AI Self-Driving Cars 135

10 Suing Automakers of AI Self-Driving Cars 143

11 Tesla Overarching FSD and AI Self-Driving Cars 151

12 Auto Repair Market and AI Self-Driving Cars 159

Appendix A: Teaching with this Material 167

Other Self-Driving Car Books by This Author 175

About the Author 233

Addendum 234

Lance B. Eliot

ACKNOWLEDGMENTS

I have been the beneficiary of advice and counsel by many friends, colleagues, family, investors, and many others. I want to thank everyone that has aided me throughout my career. I write from the heart and the head, having experienced first-hand what it means to have others around you that support you during the good times and the tough times.

To Warren Bennis, one of my doctoral advisors and ultimately a colleague, I offer my deepest thanks and appreciation, especially for his calm and insightful wisdom and support.

To Mark Stevens and his generous efforts toward funding and supporting the USC Stevens Center for Innovation.

To Lloyd Greif and the USC Lloyd Greif Center for Entrepreneurial Studies for their ongoing encouragement of founders and entrepreneurs.

To Peter Drucker, William Wang, Aaron Levie, Peter Kim, Jon Kraft, Cindy Crawford, Jenny Ming, Steve Milligan, Chis Underwood, Frank Gehry, Buzz Aldrin, Steve Forbes, Bill Thompson, Dave Dillon, Alan Fuerstman, Larry Ellison, Jim Sinegal, John Sperling, Mark Stevenson, Anand Nallathambi, Thomas Barrack, Jr., and many other innovators and leaders that I have met and gained mightily from doing so.

Thanks to Ed Trainor, Kevin Anderson, James Hickey, Wendell Jones, Ken Harris, DuWayne Peterson, Mike Brown, Jim Thornton, Abhi Beniwal, Al Biland, John Nomura, Eliot Weinman, John Desmond, and many others for their unwavering support during my career.

And most of all thanks as always to Lauren and Michael, for their ongoing support and for having seen me writing and heard much of this material during the many months involved in writing it. To their patience and willingness to listen.

Lance B. Eliot

INTRODUCTION

This is a book that provides the newest innovations and the latest Artificial Intelligence (AI) advances about the emerging nature of AI-based autonomous self-driving driverless cars. Via recent advances in Artificial Intelligence (AI) and Machine Learning (ML), we are nearing the day when vehicles can control themselves and will not require and nor rely upon human intervention to perform their driving tasks (or, that <u>allow</u> for human intervention, but only *require* human intervention in very limited ways).

Similar to my other related books, which I describe in a moment and list the chapters in the Appendix A of this book, I am particularly focused on those advances that pertain to self-driving cars. The phrase "autonomous vehicles" is often used to refer to any kind of vehicle, whether it is ground-based or in the air or sea, and whether it is a cargo hauling trailer truck or a conventional passenger car. Though the aspects described in this book are certainly applicable to all kinds of autonomous vehicles, I am focused more so here on cars.

Indeed, I am especially known for my role in aiding the advancement of self-driving cars, serving currently as the Executive Director of the Cybernetic AI Self-Driving Cars Institute.. In addition to writing software, designing and developing systems and software for self-driving cars, I also speak and write quite a bit about the topic. This book is a collection of some of my more advanced essays. For those of you that might have seen my essays posted elsewhere, I have updated them and integrated them into this book as one handy cohesive package.

You might be interested in companion books that I have written that provide additional key innovations and fundamentals about self-driving cars. Those books are entitled **"Introduction to Driverless Self-Driving Cars," "Advances in AI and Autonomous Vehicles: Cybernetic Self-Driving Cars," "Self-Driving Cars: "The Mother of All AI Projects," "Innovation and Thought Leadership on Self-Driving Driverless Cars," "New Advances in AI Autonomous Driverless Self-Driving Cars," "Autonomous Vehicle Driverless Self-Driving Cars and Artificial Intelligence," "Transformative Artificial Intelligence**

Driverless Self-Driving Cars," "Disruptive Artificial Intelligence and Driverless Self-Driving Cars, and "State-of-the-Art AI Driverless Self-Driving Cars," and "Top Trends in AI Self-Driving Cars," and "AI Innovations and Self-Driving Cars," "Crucial Advances for AI Driverless Cars," "Sociotechnical Insights and AI Driverless Cars," "Pioneering Advances for AI Driverless Cars" and "Leading Edge Trends for AI Driverless Cars," "The Cutting Edge of AI Autonomous Cars" and "The Next Wave of AI Self-Driving Cars" and "Revolutionary Innovations of AI Self-Driving Cars," and "AI Self-Driving Cars Breakthroughs," "Trailblazing Trends for AI Self-Driving Cars," "Ingenious Strides for AI Driverless Cars," "AI Self-Driving Cars Inventiveness," "Visionary Secrets of AI Driverless Cars," "Spearheading AI Self-Driving Cars," "Spurring AI Self-Driving Cars," "Avant-Garde AI Driverless Cars," "AI Self-Driving Cars Evolvement," "AI Driverless Cars Chrysalis," "Boosting AI Autonomous Cars" (they are all available via Amazon). Appendix A has a listing of the chapters covered.

For the introduction herein to this book, I am going to borrow my introduction from those companion books, since it does a good job of laying out the landscape of self-driving cars and my overall viewpoints on the topic. The remainder of the book is all new material that does not appear in the companion books.

INTRODUCTION TO SELF-DRIVING CARS

This is a book about self-driving cars. Someday in the future, we'll all have self-driving cars and this book will perhaps seem antiquated, but right now, we are at the forefront of the self-driving car wave. Daily news bombards us with flashes of new announcements by one car maker or another and leaves the impression that within the next few weeks or maybe months that the self-driving car will be here. A casual non-technical reader would assume from these news flashes that in fact we must be on the cusp of a true self-driving car. Here's a real news flash: We are still quite a distance from having a true self-driving car. It is years to go before we get there.

Why is that? Because a true self-driving car is akin to a moonshot. In the same manner that getting us to the moon was an incredible feat, likewise is achieving a true self-driving car. Anybody that suggests or even brashly states that the true self-driving car is nearly here should be viewed with great skepticism. Indeed, you'll see that I often tend to use the word "hogwash" or "crock" when I assess much of the decidedly *fake news* about self-driving cars. Those of us on the inside know that what is often reported to the outside is malarkey. Few of the insiders are willing to say so. I have no such hesitation.

Indeed, I've been writing a popular blog post about self-driving cars and hitting hard on those that try to wave their hands and pretend that we are on the imminent verge of true self-driving cars. For many years, I've been known as the AI Insider. Besides writing about AI, I also develop AI software. I do what I describe. It also gives me insights into what others that are doing AI are really doing versus what it is said they are doing.

Many faithful readers had asked me to pull together my insightful short essays and put them into another book, which you are now holding.

For those of you that have been reading my essays over the years, this collection not only puts them together into one handy package, I also updated the essays and added new material. For those of you that are new to the topic of self-driving cars and AI, I hope you find these essays approachable and informative. I also tend to have a writing style with a bit of a voice, and so you'll see that I am times have a wry sense of humor and poke at conformity.

As a former professor and founder of an AI research lab, I for many years wrote in the formal language of academic writing. I published in referred journals and served as an editor for several AI journals. This writing here is not of the nature, and I have adopted a different and more informal style for these essays. That being said, I also do mention from time-to-time more rigorous material on AI and encourage you all to dig into those deeper and more formal materials if so interested.

I am also an AI practitioner. This means that I write AI software for a living. Currently, I head-up the Cybernetics Self-Driving Car Institute, where we are developing AI software for self-driving cars. I am excited to also report that my son, also a software engineer, heads-up our Cybernetics Self-Driving Car Lab. What I have helped to start, and for which he is an integral part, ultimately he will carry long into the future after I have retired. My daughter, a marketing whiz, also is integral to our efforts as head of our Marketing group. She too will carry forward the legacy now being formulated.

For those of you that are reading this book and have a penchant for writing code, you might consider taking a look at the open source code available for self-driving cars. This is a handy place to start learning how to develop AI for self-driving cars. There are also many new educational courses spring forth. There is a growing body of those wanting to learn about and develop self-driving cars, and a growing body of colleges, labs, and other avenues by which you can learn about self-driving cars.

This book will provide a foundation of aspects that I think will get you ready for those kinds of more advanced training opportunities. If you've already taken those classes, you'll likely find these essays especially interesting as they offer a perspective that I am betting few other instructors or faculty offered to you. These are challenging essays that ask you to think beyond the conventional about self-driving cars.

THE MOTHER OF ALL AI PROJECTS

In June 2017, Apple CEO Tim Cook came out and finally admitted that Apple has been working on a self-driving car. As you'll see in my essays, Apple was enmeshed in secrecy about their self-driving car efforts. We have only been able to read the tea leaves and guess at what Apple has been up to. The notion of an iCar has been floating for quite a while, and self-driving engineers and researchers have been signing tight-lipped Non-Disclosure Agreements (NDA's) to work on projects at Apple that were as shrouded in mystery as any military invasion plans might be.

Tim Cook said something that many others in the Artificial Intelligence (AI) field have been saying, namely, the creation of a self-driving car has got to be the mother of all AI projects. In other words, it is in fact a tremendous moonshot for AI. If a self-driving car can be crafted and the AI works as we hope, it means that we have made incredible strides with AI and that therefore it opens many other worlds of potential breakthrough accomplishments that AI can solve.

Is this hyperbole? Am I just trying to make AI seem like a miracle worker and so provide self-aggrandizing statements for those of us writing the AI software for self-driving cars? No, it is not hyperbole. Developing a true self-driving car is really, really, really hard to do. Let me take a moment to explain why. As a side note, I realize that the Apple CEO is known for at times uttering hyperbole, and he had previously said for example that the year 2012 was "the mother of all years," and he had said that the release of iOS 10 was "the mother of all releases" – all of which does suggest he likes to use the handy "mother of" expression. But, I assure you, in terms of true self-driving cars, he has hit the nail on the head. For sure.

When you think about a moonshot and how we got to the moon, there are some identifiable characteristics and those same aspects can be applied to creating a true self-driving car. You'll notice that I keep putting the word "true" in front of the self-driving car expression. I do so because as per my essay about the various levels of self-driving cars, there are some self-driving cars that are only somewhat of a self-driving car. The somewhat versions are ones that require a human driver to be ready to intervene. In my view, that's not a true self-driving car. A true self-driving car is one that requires no human driver intervention at all. It is a car that can entirely undertake via automation the driving task without any human driver needed. This is the essence of what is known as a Level 5 self-driving car. We are currently at the Level 2 and Level 3 mark, and not yet at Level 5.

Getting to the moon involved aspects such as having big stretch goals, incremental progress, experimentation, innovation, and so on. Let's review how this applied to the moonshot of the bygone era, and how it applies to the self-driving car moonshot of today.

Big Stretch Goal

Trying to take a human and deliver the human to the moon, and bring them back, safely, was an extremely large stretch goal at the time. No one knew whether it could be done. The technology wasn't available yet. The cost was huge. The determination would need to be fierce. Etc. To reach a Level 5 self-driving car is going to be the same. It is a big stretch goal. We can readily get to the Level 3, and we are able to see the Level 4 just up ahead, but a Level 5 is still an unknown as to if it is doable. It should eventually be doable and in the same way that we thought we'd eventually get to the moon, but when it will occur is a different story.

Incremental Progress

Getting to the moon did not happen overnight in one fell swoop. It took years and years of incremental progress to get there. Likewise for self-driving cars. Google has famously been striving to get to the Level 5, and pretty much been willing to forgo dealing with the intervening levels, but most of the other self-driving car makers are doing the incremental route. Let's get a good Level 2 and a somewhat Level 3 going. Then, let's improve the Level 3 and get a somewhat Level 4 going. Then, let's improve the Level 4 and finally arrive at a Level 5. This seems to be the prevalent way that we are going to achieve the true self-driving car.

Experimentation

You likely know that there were various experiments involved in perfecting the approach and technology to get to the moon. As per making incremental progress, we first tried to see if we could get a rocket to go into space and safety return, then put a monkey in there, then with a human, then we went all the way to the moon but didn't land, and finally we arrived at the mission that actually landed on the moon. Self-driving cars are the same way. We are doing simulations of self-driving cars. We do testing of self-driving cars on private land under controlled situations. We do testing of self-driving cars on public roadways, often having to meet regulatory requirements including for example having an engineer or equivalent in the car to take over the controls if needed. And so on. Experiments big and small are needed to figure out what works and what doesn't.

Innovation

There are already some advances in AI that are allowing us to progress toward self-driving cars. We are going to need even more advances. Innovation in all aspects of technology are going to be required to achieve a true self-driving car. By no means do we already have everything in-hand that we need to get there. Expect new inventions and new approaches, new algorithms, etc.

Setbacks

Most of the pundits are avoiding talking about potential setbacks in the progress toward self-driving cars. Getting to the moon involved many setbacks, some of which you never have heard of and were buried at the time so as to not dampen enthusiasm and funding for getting to the moon. A recurring theme in many of my included essays is that there are going to be setbacks as we try to arrive at a true self-driving car. Take a deep breath and be ready. I just hope the setbacks don't completely stop progress. I am sure that it will cause progress to alter in a manner that we've not yet seen in the self-driving car field. I liken the self-driving car of today to the excitement everyone had for Uber when it first got going. Today, we have a different view of Uber and with each passing day there are more regulations to the ride sharing business and more concerns raised. The darling child only stays a darling until finally that child acts up. It will happen the same with self-driving cars.

SELF-DRIVING CARS CHALLENGES

But what exactly makes things so hard to have a true self-driving car, you might be asking. You have seen cruise control for years and years. You've lately seen cars that can do parallel parking. You've seen YouTube videos of Tesla drivers that put their hands out the window as their car zooms along the highway, and seen to therefore be in a self-driving car. Aren't we just needing to put a few more sensors onto a car and then we'll have in-hand a true self-driving car? Nope.

Consider for a moment the nature of the driving task. We don't just let anyone at any age drive a car. Worldwide, most countries won't license a driver until the age of 18, though many do allow a learner's permit at the age of 15 or 16. Some suggest that a younger age would be physically too small to reach the controls of the car. Though this might be the case, we could easily adjust the controls to allow for younger aged and thus smaller stature. It's not their physical size that matters. It's their cognitive development that matters.

To drive a car, you need to be able to reason about the car, what the car can and cannot do. You need to know how to operate the car. You need to know about how other cars on the road drive. You need to know what is allowed in driving such as speed limits and driving within marked lanes. You need to be able to react to situations and be able to avoid getting into accidents. You need to ascertain when to hit your brakes, when to steer clear of a pedestrian, and how to keep from ramming that motorcyclist that just cut you off.

Many of us had taken courses on driving. We studied about driving and took driver training. We had to take a test and pass it to be able to drive. The point being that though most adults take the driving task for granted, and we often "mindlessly" drive our cars, there is a significant amount of cognitive effort that goes into driving a car. After a while, it becomes second nature. You don't especially think about how you drive, you just do it. But, if you watch a novice driver, say a teenager learning to drive, you suddenly realize that there is a lot more complexity to it than we seem to realize.

Furthermore, driving is a very serious task. I recall when my daughter and son first learned to drive. They are both very conscientious people. They wanted to make sure that whatever they did, they did well, and that they did not harm anyone. Every day, when you get into a car, it is probably around 4,000 pounds of hefty metal and plastics (about two tons), and it is a lethal weapon. Think about it. You drive down the street in an object that weighs two tons and with the engine it can accelerate and ram into anything you want to hit. The damage a car can inflict is very scary. Both my children were surprised that they were being given the right to maneuver this monster of a beast that could cause tremendous harm entirely by merely letting go of the steering wheel for a moment or taking your eyes off the road.

In fact, in the United States alone there are about 30,000 deaths per year by auto accidents, which is around 100 per day. Given that there are about 263 million cars in the United States, I am actually more amazed that the number of fatalities is not a lot higher. During my morning commute, I look at all the thousands of cars on the freeway around me, and I think that if all of them decided to go zombie and drive in a crazy maniac way, there would be many people dead. Somehow, incredibly, each day, most people drive relatively safely. To me, that's a miracle right there. Getting millions and millions of people to be safe and sane when behind the wheel of a two ton mobile object, it's a feat that we as a society should admire with pride.

So, hopefully you are in agreement that the driving task requires a great deal of cognition. You don't' need to be especially smart to drive a car, and we've done quite a bit to make car driving viable for even the average dolt. There isn't an IQ test that you need to take to drive a car. If you can read and write, and pass a test, you pretty much can legally drive a car. There are of course some that drive a car and are not legally permitted to do so, plus there are private areas such as farms where drivers are young, but for public roadways in the United States, you can be generally of average intelligence (or less) and be able to legally drive.

This though makes it seem like the cognitive effort must not be much. If the cognitive effort was truly hard, wouldn't we only have Einstein's that could drive a car? We have made sure to keep the driving task as simple as we can, by making the controls easy and relatively standardized, and by having roads that are relatively standardized, and so on. It is as though Disneyland has put their Autopia into the real-world, by us all as a society agreeing that roads will be a certain way, and we'll all abide by the various rules of driving.

A modest cognitive task by a human is still something that stymies AI. You certainly know that AI has been able to beat chess players and be good at other kinds of games. This type of narrow cognition is not what car driving is about. Car driving is much wider. It requires knowledge about the world, which a chess playing AI system does not need to know. The cognitive aspects of driving are on the one hand seemingly simple, but at the same time require layer upon layer of knowledge about cars, people, roads, rules, and a myriad of other "common sense" aspects. We don't have any AI systems today that have that same kind of breadth and depth of awareness and knowledge.

As revealed in my essays, the self-driving car of today is using trickery to do particular tasks. It is all very narrow in operation. Plus, it currently assumes that a human driver is ready to intervene. It is like a child that we have taught to stack blocks, but we are needed to be right there in case the child stacks them too high and they begin to fall over. AI of today is brittle, it is narrow, and it does not approach the cognitive abilities of humans. This is why the true self-driving car is somewhere out in the future.

Another aspect to the driving task is that it is not solely a mind exercise. You do need to use your senses to drive. You use your eyes a vision sensors to see the road ahead. You vision capability is like a streaming video, which your brain needs to continually analyze as you drive. Where is the road? Is there a pedestrian in the way? Is there another car ahead of you? Your senses are relying a flood of info to your brain. Self-driving cars are trying to do the same, by using cameras, radar, ultrasound, and lasers. This is an attempt at mimicking how humans have senses and sensory apparatus.

Thus, the driving task is mental and physical. You use your senses, you use your arms and legs to manipulate the controls of the car, and you use your brain to assess the sensory info and direct your limbs to act upon the controls of the car. This all happens instantly. If you've ever perhaps gotten something in your eye and only had one eye available to drive with, you suddenly realize how dependent upon vision you are. If you have a broken foot with a cast, you suddenly realize how hard it is to control the brake pedal and the accelerator. If you've taken medication and your brain is maybe sluggish, you suddenly realize how much mental strain is required to drive a car.

An AI system that plays chess only needs to be focused on playing chess. The physical aspects aren't important because usually a human moves the chess pieces or the chessboard is shown on an electronic display. Using AI for a more life-and-death task such as analyzing MRI images of patients, this again does not require physical capabilities and instead is done by examining images of bits.

Driving a car is a true life-and-death task. It is a use of AI that can easily and at any moment produce death. For those colleagues of mine that are developing this AI, as am I, we need to keep in mind the somber aspects of this. We are producing software that will have in its virtual hands the lives of the occupants of the car, and the lives of those in other nearby cars, and the lives of nearby pedestrians, etc. Chess is not usually a life-or-death matter.

Driving is all around us. Cars are everywhere. Most of today's AI applications involve only a small number of people. Or, they are behind the scenes and we as humans have other recourse if the AI messes up. AI that is driving a car at 80 miles per hour on a highway had better not mess up. The consequences are grave. Multiply this by the number of cars, if we could put magically self-driving into every car in the USA, we'd have AI running in the 263 million cars. That's a lot of AI spread around. This is AI on a massive scale that we are not doing today and that offers both promise and potential peril.

There are some that want AI for self-driving cars because they envision a world without any car accidents. They envision a world in which there is no car congestion and all cars cooperate with each other. These are wonderful utopian visions.

They are also very misleading. The adoption of self-driving cars is going to be incremental and not overnight. We cannot economically just junk all existing cars. Nor are we going to be able to affordably retrofit existing cars. It is more likely that self-driving cars will be built into new cars and that over many years of gradual replacement of existing cars that we'll see the mix of self-driving cars become substantial in the real-world.

In these essays, I have tried to offer technological insights without being overly technical in my description, and also blended the business, societal, and economic aspects too. Technologists need to consider the non-technological impacts of what they do. Non-technologists should be aware of what is being developed.

We all need to work together to collectively be prepared for the enormous disruption and transformative aspects of true self-driving cars. We all need to be involved in this mother of all AI projects.

WHAT THIS BOOK PROVIDES

What does this book provide to you? It introduces many of the key elements about self-driving cars and does so with an AI based perspective. I weave together technical and non-technical aspects, readily going from being concerned about the cognitive capabilities of the driving task and how the technology is embodying this into self-driving cars, and in the next breath I discuss the societal and economic aspects.

They are all intertwined because that's the way reality is. You cannot separate out the technology per se, and instead must consider it within the milieu of what is being invented and innovated, and do so with a mindset towards the contemporary mores and culture that shape what we are doing and what we hope to do.

WHY THIS BOOK

I wrote this book to try and bring to the public view many aspects about self-driving cars that nobody seems to be discussing.

For business leaders that are either involved in making self-driving cars or that are going to leverage self-driving cars, I hope that this book will enlighten you as to the risks involved and ways in which you should be strategizing about how to deal with those risks.

For entrepreneurs, startups and other businesses that want to enter into the self-driving car market that is emerging, I hope this book sparks your interest in doing so, and provides some sense of what might be prudent to pursue.

For researchers that study self-driving cars, I hope this book spurs your interest in the risks and safety issues of self-driving cars, and also nudges you toward conducting research on those aspects.

For students in computer science or related disciplines, I hope this book will provide you with interesting and new ideas and material, for which you might conduct research or provide some career direction insights for you.

For AI companies and high-tech companies pursuing self-driving cars, this book will hopefully broaden your view beyond just the mere coding and development needed to make self-driving cars.

For all readers, I hope that you will find the material in this book to be stimulating. Some of it will be repetitive of things you already know. But I am pretty sure that you'll also find various eureka moments whereby you'll discover a new technique or approach that you had not earlier thought of. I am also betting that there will be material that forces you to rethink some of your current practices.

I am not saying you will suddenly have an epiphany and change what you are doing. I do think though that you will reconsider or perhaps revisit what you are doing.

For anyone choosing to use this book for teaching purposes, please take a look at my suggestions for doing so, as described in the Appendix. I have found the material handy in courses that I have taught, and likewise other faculty have told me that they have found the material handy, in some cases as extended readings and in other instances as a core part of their course (depending on the nature of the class).

In my writing for this book, I have tried carefully to blend both the practitioner and the academic styles of writing. It is not as dense as is typical academic journal writing, but at the same time offers depth by going into the nuances and trade-offs of various practices.

The word "deep" is in vogue today, meaning getting deeply into a subject or topic, and so is the word "unpack" which means to tease out the underlying aspects of a subject or topic. I have sought to offer material that addresses an issue or topic by going relatively deeply into it and make sure that it is well unpacked.

In any book about AI, it is difficult to use our everyday words without having some of them be misinterpreted. Specifically, it is easy to anthropomorphize AI. When I say that an AI system "knows" something, I do not want you to construe that the AI system has sentience and "knows" in the same way that humans do. They aren't that way, as yet. I have tried to use quotes around such words from time-to-time to emphasize that the words I am using should not be misinterpreted to ascribe true human intelligence to the AI systems that we know of today. If I used quotes around all such words, the book would be very difficult to read, and so I am doing so judiciously. Please keep that in mind as you read the material, thanks.

Some of the material is time-based in terms of covering underway activities, and though some of it might decay, nonetheless I believe you'll find the material useful and informative.

COMPANION BOOKS

If you find this material of interest, you might enjoy these too:

1. **"Introduction to Driverless Self-Driving Cars"** by Dr. Lance Eliot

2. **"Innovation and Thought Leadership on Self-Driving Driverless Cars"** by Dr. Lance Eliot

3. **"Advances in AI and Autonomous Vehicles: Cybernetic Self-Driving Cars"** by Dr. Lance Eliot

4. **"Self-Driving Cars: The Mother of All AI Projects"** by Dr. Lance Eliot

5. **"New Advances in AI Autonomous Driverless Self-Driving Cars"** by Dr. Lance Eliot

6. **"Autonomous Vehicle Driverless Self-Driving Cars and Artificial Intelligence"** by Dr. Lance Eliot and Michael B. Eliot

7. **"Transformative Artificial Intelligence Driverless Self-Driving Cars"** by Dr. Lance Eliot

8. **"Disruptive Artificial Intelligence and Driverless Self-Driving Cars"** by Dr. Lance Eliot

9. "State-of-the-Art AI Driverless Self-Driving Cars" by Dr. Lance Eliot

10. "**Top Trends in AI Self-Driving Cars**" by Dr. Lance Eliot

11. **"AI Innovations and Self-Driving Cars"** by Dr. Lance Eliot

12. **"Crucial Advances for AI Driverless Cars"** by Dr. Lance Eliot

13. **"Sociotechnical Insights and AI Driverless Cars"** by Dr. Lance Eliot.

14. **"Pioneering Advances for AI Driverless Cars"** by Dr. Lance Eliot

15. **"Leading Edge Trends for AI Driverless Cars"** by Dr. Lance Eliot

16. **"The Cutting Edge of AI Autonomous Cars"** by Dr. Lance Eliot

17. **"The Next Wave of AI Self-Driving Cars"** by Dr. Lance Eliot

18. **"Revolutionary Innovations of AI Driverless Cars"** by Dr. Lance Eliot

19. **"AI Self-Driving Cars Breakthroughs"** by Dr. Lance Eliot

20. **"Trailblazing Trends for AI Self-Driving Cars"** by Dr. Lance Eliot

21. **"Ingenious Strides for AI Driverless Cars"** by Dr. Lance Eliot

22. **"AI Self-Driving Cars Inventiveness"** by Dr. Lance Eliot

23. **"Visionary Secrets of AI Driverless Cars"** by Dr. Lance Eliot

24. **"Spearheading AI Self-Driving Cars"** by Dr. Lance Eliot

25. **"Spurring AI Self-Driving Cars"** by Dr. Lance Eliot

26. **"Avant-Garde AI Driverless Cars"** by Dr. Lance Eliot

27. **"AI Self-Driving Cars Evolvement"** by Dr. Lance Eliot

28. **"AI Driverless Cars Chrysalis"** by Dr. Lance Eliot

29. **"Boosting AI Autonomous Cars"** by Dr. Lance Eliot

These books are available on Amazon and at other major global booksellers.

CHAPTER 1

ELIOT FRAMEWORK FOR AI SELF-DRIVING CARS

CHAPTER 1

ELIOT FRAMEWORK FOR AI SELF-DRIVING CARS

This chapter is a core foundational aspect for understanding AI self-driving cars and I have used this same chapter in several of my other books to introduce the reader to essential elements of this field. Once you've read this chapter, you'll be prepared to read the rest of the material since the foundational essence of the components of autonomous AI driverless self-driving cars will have been established for you.

―――――――――

When I give presentations about self-driving cars and teach classes on the topic, I have found it helpful to provide a framework around which the various key elements of self-driving cars can be understood and organized (see diagram at the end of this chapter). The framework needs to be simple enough to convey the overarching elements, but at the same time not so simple that it belies the true complexity of self-driving cars. As such, I am going to describe the framework here and try to offer in a thousand words (or more!) what the framework diagram itself intends to portray.

The core elements on the diagram are numbered for ease of reference. The numbering does not suggest any kind of prioritization of the elements. Each element is crucial. Each element has a purpose, and otherwise would not be included in the framework. For some self-driving cars, a particular element might be more important or somehow distinguished in comparison to other self-driving cars.

You could even use the framework to rate a particular self-driving car, doing so by gauging how well it performs in each of the elements of the framework. I will describe each of the elements, one at a time. After doing so, I'll discuss aspects that illustrate how the elements interact and perform during the overall effort of a self-driving car.

At the Cybernetic Self-Driving Car Institute, we use the framework to keep track of what we are working on, and how we are developing software that fills in what is needed to achieve Level 5 self-driving cars.

D-01: Sensor Capture

Let's start with the one element that often gets the most attention in the press about self-driving cars, namely, the sensory devices for a self-driving car.

On the framework, the box labeled as D-01 indicates "Sensor Capture" and refers to the processes of the self-driving car that involve collecting data from the myriad of sensors that are used for a self-driving car. The types of devices typically involved are listed, such as the use of mono cameras, stereo cameras, LIDAR devices, radar systems, ultrasonic devices, GPS, IMU, and so on.

These devices are tasked with obtaining data about the status of the self-driving car and the world around it. Some of the devices are continually providing updates, while others of the devices await an indication by the self-driving car that the device is supposed to collect data. The data might be first transformed in some fashion by the device itself, or it might instead be fed directly into the sensor capture as raw data. At that point, it might be up to the sensor capture processes to do transformations on the data. This all varies depending upon the nature of the devices being used and how the devices were designed and developed.

D-02: Sensor Fusion

Imagine that your eyeballs receive visual images, your nose receives odors, your ears receive sounds, and in essence each of your distinct sensory devices is getting some form of input. The input befits the nature of the device. Likewise, for a self-driving car, the cameras provide visual images, the radar returns radar reflections, and so on.

Each device provides the data as befits what the device does.

At some point, using the analogy to humans, you need to merge together what your eyes see, what your nose smells, what your ears hear, and piece it all together into a larger sense of what the world is all about and what is happening around you. Sensor fusion is the action of taking the singular aspects from each of the devices and putting them together into a larger puzzle.

Sensor fusion is a tough task. There are some devices that might not be working at the time of the sensor capture. Or, there might some devices that are unable to report well what they have detected. Again, using a human analogy, suppose you are in a dark room and so your eyes cannot see much. At that point, you might need to rely more so on your ears and what you hear. The same is true for a self-driving car. If the cameras are obscured due to snow and sleet, it might be that the radar can provide a greater indication of what the external conditions consist of.

In the case of a self-driving car, there can be a plethora of such sensory devices. Each is reporting what it can. Each might have its difficulties. Each might have its limitations, such as how far ahead it can detect an object. All of these limitations need to be considered during the sensor fusion task.

D-03: Virtual World Model

For humans, we presumably keep in our minds a model of the world around us when we are driving a car. In your mind, you know that the car is going at say 60 miles per hour and that you are on a freeway. You have a model in your mind that your car is surrounded by other cars, and that there are lanes to the freeway. Your model is not only based on what you can see, hear, etc., but also what you know about the nature of the world. You know that at any moment that car ahead of you can smash on its brakes, or the car behind you can ram into your car, or that the truck in the next lane might swerve into your lane.

The AI of the self-driving car needs to have a virtual world model, which it then keeps updated with whatever it is receiving from the sensor fusion, which received its input from the sensor capture and the sensory devices.

D-04: System Action Plan

By having a virtual world model, the AI of the self-driving car is able to keep track of where the car is and what is happening around the car. In addition, the AI needs to determine what to do next. Should the self-driving car hit its brakes? Should the self-driving car stay in its lane or swerve into the lane to the left? Should the self-driving car accelerate or slow down?

A system action plan needs to be prepared by the AI of the self-driving car. The action plan specifies what actions should be taken. The actions need to pertain to the status of the virtual world model. Plus, the actions need to be realizable.

This realizability means that the AI cannot just assert that the self-driving car should suddenly sprout wings and fly. Instead, the AI must be bound by whatever the self-driving car can actually do, such as coming to a halt in a distance of X feet at a speed of Y miles per hour, rather than perhaps asserting that the self-driving car come to a halt in 0 feet as though it could instantaneously come to a stop while it is in motion.

D-05: Controls Activation

The system action plan is implemented by activating the controls of the car to act according to what the plan stipulates. This might mean that the accelerator control is commanded to increase the speed of the car. Or, the steering control is commanded to turn the steering wheel 30 degrees to the left or right.

One question arises as to whether or not the controls respond as they are commanded to do. In other words, suppose the AI has commanded the accelerator to increase, but for some reason it does not do so. Or, maybe it tries to do so, but the speed of the car does not increase. The controls activation feeds back into the virtual world model, and simultaneously the virtual world model is getting updated from the sensors, the sensor capture, and the sensor fusion. This allows the AI to ascertain what has taken place as a result of the controls being commanded to take some kind of action.

By the way, please keep in mind that though the diagram seems to have a linear progression to it, the reality is that these are all aspects of the self-driving car that are happening in parallel and simultaneously. The sensors are capturing data, meanwhile the sensor fusion is taking place, meanwhile the virtual model is being updated, meanwhile the system action plan is being formulated and reformulated, meanwhile the controls are being activated.

This is the same as a human being that is driving a car. They are eyeballing the road, meanwhile they are fusing in their mind the sights, sounds, etc., meanwhile their mind is updating their model of the world around them, meanwhile they are formulating an action plan of what to do, and meanwhile they are pushing their foot onto the pedals and steering the car. In the normal course of driving a car, you are doing all of these at once. I mention this so that when you look at the diagram, you will think of the boxes as processes that are all happening at the same time, and not as though only one happens and then the next.

They are shown diagrammatically in a simplistic manner to help comprehend what is taking place. You though should also realize that they are working in parallel and simultaneous with each other. This is a tough aspect in that the inter-element communications involve latency and other aspects that must be taken into account. There can be delays in one element updating and then sharing its latest status with other elements.

D-06: Automobile & CAN

Contemporary cars use various automotive electronics and a Controller Area Network (CAN) to serve as the components that underlie the driving aspects of a car. There are Electronic Control Units (ECU's) which control subsystems of the car, such as the engine, the brakes, the doors, the windows, and so on.

The elements D-01, D-02, D-03, D-04, D-05 are layered on top of the D-06, and must be aware of the nature of what the D-06 is able to do and not do.

D-07: In-Car Commands

Humans are going to be occupants in self-driving cars. In a Level 5 self-driving car, there must be some form of communication that takes place between the humans and the self-driving car. For example, I go into a self-driving car and tell it that I want to be driven over to Disneyland, and along the way I want to stop at In-and-Out Burger. The self-driving car now parses what I've said and tries to then establish a means to carry out my wishes.

In-car commands can happen at any time during a driving journey. Though my example was about an in-car command when I first got into my self-driving car, it could be that while the self-driving car is carrying out the journey that I change my mind. Perhaps after getting stuck in traffic, I tell the self-driving car to forget about getting the burgers and just head straight over to the theme park. The self-driving car needs to be alert to in-car commands throughout the journey.

D-08: V2X Communications

We will ultimately have self-driving cars communicating with each other, doing so via V2V (Vehicle-to-Vehicle) communications. We will also have self-driving cars that communicate with the roadways and other aspects of the transportation infrastructure, doing so via V2I (Vehicle-to-Infrastructure).

The variety of ways in which a self-driving car will be communicating with other cars and infrastructure is being called V2X, whereby the letter X means whatever else we identify as something that a car should or would want to communicate with. The V2X communications will be taking place simultaneous with everything else on the diagram, and those other elements will need to incorporate whatever it gleans from those V2X communications.

D-09: Deep Learning

The use of Deep Learning permeates all other aspects of the self-driving car. The AI of the self-driving car will be using deep learning to do a better job at the systems action plan, and at the controls activation, and at the sensor fusion, and so on.

Currently, the use of artificial neural networks is the most prevalent form of deep learning. Based on large swaths of data, the neural networks attempt to "learn" from the data and therefore direct the efforts of the self-driving car accordingly.

D-10: Tactical AI

Tactical AI is the element of dealing with the moment-to-moment driving of the self-driving car. Is the self-driving car staying in its lane of the freeway? Is the car responding appropriately to the controls commands? Are the sensory devices working?

For human drivers, the tactical equivalent can be seen when you watch a novice driver such as a teenager that is first driving. They are focused on the mechanics of the driving task, keeping their eye on the road while also trying to properly control the car.

D-11: Strategic AI

The Strategic AI aspects of a self-driving car are dealing with the larger picture of what the self-driving car is trying to do. If I had asked that the self-driving car take me to Disneyland, there is an overall journey map that needs to be kept and maintained.

There is an interaction between the Strategic AI and the Tactical AI. The Strategic AI is wanting to keep on the mission of the driving, while the Tactical AI is focused on the particulars underway in the driving effort. If the Tactical AI seems to wander away from the overarching mission, the Strategic AI wants to see why and get things back on track. If the Tactical AI realizes that there is something amiss on the self-driving car, it needs to alert the Strategic AI accordingly and have an adjustment to the overarching mission that is underway.

D-12: Self-Aware AI

Very few of the self-driving cars being developed are including a Self-Aware AI element, which we at the Cybernetic Self-Driving Car Institute believe is crucial to Level 5 self-driving cars.

The Self-Aware AI element is intended to watch over itself, in the sense that the AI is making sure that the AI is working as intended. Suppose you had a human driving a car, and they were starting to drive erratically. Hopefully, their own self-awareness would make them realize they themselves are driving poorly, such as perhaps starting to fall asleep after having been driving for hours on end. If you had a passenger in the car, they might be able to alert the driver if the driver is starting to do something amiss. This is exactly what the Self-Aware

AI element tries to do, it becomes the overseer of the AI, and tries to detect when the AI has become faulty or confused, and then find ways to overcome the issue.

D-13: Economic

The economic aspects of a self-driving car are not per se a technology aspect of a self-driving car, but the economics do indeed impact the nature of a self-driving car. For example, the cost of outfitting a self-driving car with every kind of possible sensory device is prohibitive, and so choices need to be made about which devices are used. And, for those sensory devices chosen, whether they would have a full set of features or a more limited set of features.

We are going to have self-driving cars that are at the low-end of a consumer cost point, and others at the high-end of a consumer cost point. You cannot expect that the self-driving car at the low-end is going to be as robust as the one at the high-end. I realize that many of the self-driving car pundits are acting as though all self-driving cars will be the same, but they won't be. Just like anything else, we are going to have self-driving cars that have a range of capabilities. Some will be better than others. Some will be safer than others. This is the way of the real-world, and so we need to be thinking about the economics aspects when considering the nature of self-driving cars.

D-14: Societal

This component encompasses the societal aspects of AI which also impacts the technology of self-driving cars. For example, the famous Trolley Problem involves what choices should a self-driving car make when faced with life-and-death matters. If the self-driving car is about to either hit a child standing in the roadway, or instead ram into a tree at the side of the road and possibly kill the humans in the self-driving car, which choice should be made?

We need to keep in mind the societal aspects will underlie the AI of the self-driving car. Whether we are aware of it explicitly or not, the AI will have embedded into it various societal assumptions.

D-15: Innovation

I included the notion of innovation into the framework because we can anticipate that whatever a self-driving car consists of, it will continue to be innovated over time. The self-driving cars coming out in the next several years will undoubtedly be different and less innovative than the versions that come out in ten years hence, and so on.

Framework Overall

For those of you that want to learn about self-driving cars, you can potentially pick a particular element and become specialized in that aspect. Some engineers are focusing on the sensory devices. Some engineers focus on the controls activation. And so on. There are specialties in each of the elements.

Researchers are likewise specializing in various aspects. For example, there are researchers that are using Deep Learning to see how best it can be used for sensor fusion. There are other researchers that are using Deep Learning to derive good System Action Plans. Some are studying how to develop AI for the Strategic aspects of the driving task, while others are focused on the Tactical aspects.

A well-prepared all-around software developer that is involved in self-driving cars should be familiar with all of the elements, at least to the degree that they know what each element does. This is important since whatever piece of the pie that the software developer works on, they need to be knowledgeable about what the other elements are doing.

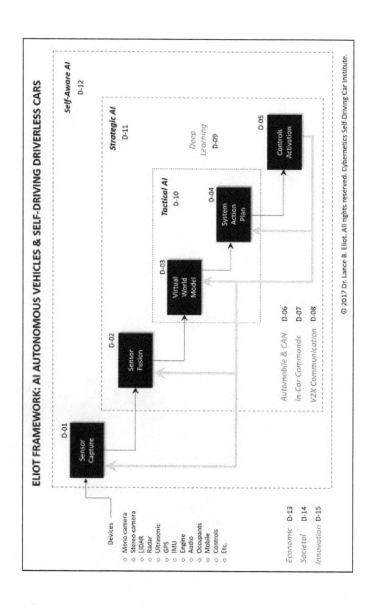

CHAPTER 2

ZERO KNOWLEDGE PROOFS AND AI SELF-DRIVING CARS

CHAPTER 2

ZERO KNOWLEDGE PROOFS
AND AI SELF-DRIVING CARS

Anyone that knows me, knows that I am a fan of spy novels and spy movies. Maybe that's why I am also fascinated by Zero Knowledge Proofs (ZKP or sometimes shortened to ZK), a type of cryptographic method of intriguing possibilities.

I recently had an opportunity to attend *ZK Day 2019* at the Simons Institute for the Theory of Computing at the University of California Berkeley, an all-day symposium entitled "Blockchains, Micropayments and Zero Knowledge." Luminaries of the field were there, and the stellar event was moderated by Dr. Shafi Goldwasser, Director of the Simons Institute and a pioneer and co-founder of the field.

Those of you in the AI field might not be particularly versed in ZKP, perhaps you have heard of it, distantly, faintly, yet you are unsure of what it consists of. I'll go ahead and provide you with a layman's explanation and include some handy references of salient works on the topic. The mathematics of ZKP can be daunting, which if you relish "pure" computer science offers a richness of a high order, while if you are less-so mathematically focused and more-so software engineering inclined, there are ways to make use of ZKP and do so by reviewing open source code and ZKP programs that are available on GitHub.

You might be already puzzled that I've said that my fascination with ZKP ties into my savoring spy stories. How do the two connect, you might be wondering?

Let's start at the beginning. Suppose you want to prove to someone that you know something, a particular something. You could just tell them the something, but in so doing, you have completely revealed it. There might be situations whereby you don't want to have to reveal the something, and yet nonetheless be able to somehow validate or "prove" that you really do know it.

Seems like a conundrum. How might I convince you that I know something, and yet not reveal the actual something in the process of doing so?

ZKP AND THE CASE OF THE SECRET PIN

This reminds me of a kind of real-world use case when I was in college getting my degree in computer science. I was working in the campus computer center to cover my tuition and admittedly would have worked for free due to my love for computer science (what, they'll pay me to develop software and help others with their programs, sign me up!). There was a bunch of us computer science types that inhabited the computer center, often toying with each other to see who could come up with the cleverest showcasing of our budding knowledge and skills.

We had a manager that worked full-time as a regular administrative job in the computer center, and she kept a tight rein on our potential antics. She had an office that was enclosed within the computer center and had windows that viewed into the area where the computer stations were provided for students doing labs. She would open her blinds when she got to work, watching us like hawks, making sure that those sometimes lazy or inattentive student-workers manning the lab were keeping on their toes (I don't blame her, a number of my co-workers would bury themselves at a workstation and not help anyone else, true to an anti-social natural nature).

One day, on a Thursday, she indicated to me that she was going on vacation the next day, and would lock-up her office, but she also realized that she kept spare equipment in her office, which might be needed while she was away camping. She told me the PIN to the numeric lock on her office door. It was quite an honor, since she seemed to distrust nearly all of us, and she was giving me the key to the kingdom, as it were.

But she also didn't want others to know that she had given me the PIN. She worried that word would spread about her doing so, and I might get picked-on for being a favored son, as they say, and she also figured that it would get me into a pickle of having to say yes or no whenever spare equipment requests might arise. All in all, she was giving me the PIN as a last resort option and for a contingency use only, which she hoped and assumed would not need to be invoked while she was gone for just one measly day.

Friday morning, I came into the computer center, and was immediately confronted by a pal of mine. He had heard a rumor that the manager had given me the PIN. He was flabbergasted. Why didn't he get the PIN? The idea of my having the PIN was so outlandish that he dismissed the rumor entirely. It made no sense to him that I would have the vaunted PIN.

I realize that I probably should have remained mum, but, hey, I felt that my honor was at stake, namely why couldn't I have been chosen to have the PIN? So, I whispered to him quietly, and swore him to utter secrecy, yes, I did indeed possess the PIN. It was locked away in my mind, like a steel vault, never to be opened, never to be revealed.

Of course, he did not believe me. I was saying that I had the PIN to merely fuel the rumors and to make myself look important, at least that's what he retorted. We are now at the crucial point of my story.

Are you ready?

Prove it, he said.

How was I to prove that I had the PIN? I could have told him the PIN number straight out, but I had been sworn to keep it private and only I was to have it. Telling him the PIN was not the way to go.

I could have walked him over to her door, which was on the other side of the lab area and not readily visible and used the PIN to open the door. He might though get a glance of the PIN, and I didn't want that to happen. Also, he would be able to later on tattletale to the manager and say that I had actually shown him my entering into her office. Something that might have gotten me fired from my dream job.

Here's what I did. I told him to wait right where he was. He could see the windows of her office and the blinds were closed, since she was not present in the office. I instructed him to carefully watch the windows of her office.

I then walked around to where her office door was, let myself into her office, quietly, unseen, and turned on the lights. I left them on for about ten seconds, and then turned them off. I snuck out of her office, making sure that I had not been observed.

When I got back to my pal, I asked him what he had seen. He reported that the lights in her office had come on and then gone off. It was me, I did it, I explained. This was my proof that I had the PIN.

He pondered this. Well, it was the case that the manager wasn't at work, and it was the case that I had seemingly disappeared for a few moments, and it was the case that the lights mysteriously came on and went off, which logically should not have occurred, therefore my claim was plausible.

Notice that I had not told him the PIN number. He could have asked me about the PIN number, such as how many digits in length it is, which might have been a means for me to try and prove that I knew the PIN, but if I told him the number of digits, it would be tantamount to giving a clue about the PIN. I did not want to tell him the PIN and nor provide any clues whatsoever about the PIN.

I had wanted to provide zero-knowledge about the PIN, not even a scrap of knowledge about it.

I had wanted to provide proof-of-knowledge that I actually did know the PIN.

Thusly, I had performed a zero-knowledge proof-of-knowledge, doing so about my claimed in-hand PIN.

Since saying "zero-knowledge proof-of-knowledge" is a somewhat lengthy statement, a mouthful, we abbreviate it to simply Zero Knowledge Proof. I mention this because it can be confusing to make sense of just the three words, Zero, Knowledge, Proof, and you aren't sure what the word zero applies to and nor the word knowledge and nor the word proof. I hope you can see the sensibility of it, using the long form, it is zero-knowledge revealed, in the act of providing a proof-of-knowledge.

Wait a second, you might be saying, did my pal really believe that I had the PIN, due to the lights on and off evidence?

No, he did not. Being a suspicious person, he pointed out that I might have had an external means to turn her office lights on and off, maybe a remote button of some kind. Or, maybe it was a fluke that the lights perchance went on and off at that particular time. Or, maybe I knew beforehand that the lights were set to run on a timer and would go on and off at just that precise moment.

I shook my head. Really? I would go to that kind of trouble to falsely try to prove that I had the PIN? Well, anyway, I decided that perhaps I could deal with his doubting ways. I told him to once again wait and watch the office window. Away I went, and this time I entered in her office, using the PIN again, and twisted the blinds so they flipped one way and to the other way, doing so very fast, fast enough that no one could see into the office.

I came back to my waiting and formerly doubting pal. He admitted that it sure seemed like I must have the PIN. He had witnessed two events, one after the other, and the first one gave him a kind of probability or certainty level about my having the PIN, which got further reinforced upon my second alleged visit that flipped the blinds.

You could say that I was the Prover, having to prove something that I claimed to know. You could say that my pal was the Verifier, trying to verify the veracity of my claim that I know something. When you read the literature and research on ZKP, you'll find that it is customary to label the Prover as a thing or person labeled as "A" and the Verifier as a thing or person labeled "B" – allowing you to then portray the situation in a mathematical way of using A and B.

The letters A and B are somewhat unassuming and so there are those that like to refer to A as being "Alice" and B to being "Bob," providing a bit more catchiness to the matter. Since it might be hard to remember which is which, whether Alice is the prover or the verifier, or whether Bob is the prover of the verifier, some like to use the word "Peggy" as representing the Prover and the word "Victor" as representing the Verifier, an easier alignment of the letters that start the respective words.

You now know the rudiments of ZKP. There is a Prover that claims to have some kind of knowledge, which the Prover does not want to reveal per se, including not even offering clues that might reveal it, and there is a Verifier that is trying to assert the veracity of the Prover's claim, which the Prover then uses some kind of proof to try and convince the Verifier about the Prover's veracity.

I think you can directly discern the privacy value of such an approach.

ZKP HANDY FOR CRYPTOCURRENCIES

Take the advent of cryptocurrency as an example.

When using blockchain and a cryptocurrency such as bitcoin, the traditional approach involves making openly available the history of a given bitcoin, allowing you to trace it from its origins and to each of the times that it was spent on something.

When you ponder this, you realize that the cash you carry in your wallet or purse is not that way. Pull out a five-dollar bill. Can you tell me where it has been, prior to arriving in your hands? Not likely.

The cash you use every day is considered fungible. That five-dollar bill is the same as any other and there is no ready way to trace where any of them have come and gone. Sure, there is a minted number on the bill that you can use to identify its origins, but the path thereafter is pretty much a mystery. You likely know where you got the five-dollar bill, and when you spend it you'll know what you did with it, but anything else in-between is unknown to you and pretty much unknown to everyone else too.

In the case of cryptocurrencies, the ease of traceability comes with being digital. You might like the traceability and it gives you comfort to know where a particular cryptocurrency item has been. On the other hand, it opens the door to allow knowing who had it, what they used it for, when they used, etc.

I'm guessing you've had a moment when you were about to use on your normal credit cards, realized that by using it you could be traced, and perhaps switched over to cash, doing so to keep away prying eyes (if that's never occurred to you, perhaps I've just triggered you, sorry). Generally, any use of a "traditional" cryptocurrency is going to be similar to the notion of using a credit card that can be traced, though in some ways even less private, since your credit card info might be known mainly by your issuing bank, while the blockchain you are using might be available to anyone on planet Earth.

One of the presenters at the ZK Day event was Dr. Alessandro Chiesa, a Senior Advisor at the Simons Institute and a faculty member at UC Berkeley. He is a co-inventor of the Zerocash protocol, which endeavors to use ZKP for blockchain and cryptocurrencies. This adds a capability of privacy that otherwise is not inherent in traditional cryptocurrencies. For a handy foundational paper from 2014, which also covers the zk-SNARKS (Succinct Non-interactive Arguments of Knowledge), see: http://zerocash-project.org/media/pdf/zerocash-extended-20140518.pdf.

In terms of classic reading on ZKP, you might want to look at this groundbreaking paper that essentially got ZKP rolling: https://people.csail.mit.edu/silvio/Selected%20Scientific%20 Papers/Proof%20Systems/The_Knowledge_Complexity_Of_Interac tive_Proof_Systems.pdf The paper was co-authored by Shafi Goldwasser, Silvio Micali, and Charles Rackoff. Dr. Silvio Micali was also a presenter at the ZK Day event, providing insights about a version of blockchain called Algorand: https://www.algorand.com/.

I'll soon herein be discussing the ZKP as it applies to AI self-driving cars, and meanwhile some devoted readers will remember this piece on blockchain for AI self-driving cars that I wrote for my column: https://www.aitrends.com/selfdrivingcars/blockchain-self-driving-cars-using-p2p-distributed-ledgers-bitcoin/.

SOME MORE ZKP ASPECTS OF INTEREST

You might be anxious that so far, I have not seemingly said anything about spy novels and spy movies, yet I had promised earlier that I would connect the dots on ZKP and spy stories.

For those of you that like classic spy movies, consider the famous Alfred Hitchcock directed film entitled *Torn Curtain*.

The story takes place during the Cold War era. Actor Paul Newman plays a character named Michael Armstrong that is an American rocket scientist, and before I say anything else, PLOT SPOILER, he opts to defect to East Germany on the other side of the Iron Curtain, but it is a ruse to get him access to Professor Lindt, played by actor Ludwig Donath, in hopes of America learning a rocketry formula that Lindt has perfected. Sidenote, there is a love interest twist to the story, involving Julie Andrews playing the role of Sarah Sherman, so it's got both spying and romance, for those of you that like that cup of tea.

In any case, there is a pivotal moment in the film when finally, the American rocket scientist has a moment alone with the East German (Soviet Union, essentially) rocket scientist, occurring after all kinds of shenanigans and plot turns.

They are standing at the chalkboard that contains Lindt's secret formulas, and there is an empty space for the crucial missing link that the Americans have not been able to solve.

We are now ready for the connection to ZKP.

Lindt asks the American rocket scientist, Michael Armstrong, to fill-in the missing piece. He does so. Say what, have the Americans just given the missing secret away? Well, Lindt immediately tells Michael Armstrong that the missing piece shown will not work. Michael Armstrong insists that it does. This gets Lindt into a dander, and he erases the formula portion written by the American, and proudly shows him the right missing piece, the one that Lindt had discovered. Oops, bad news for Lindt, he has just revealed the secret to the American. The rest of the movie involves the American rocket scientist trying to get away with the new knowledge embedded in his mind and bring it back to the USA.

Lindt was fooled into giving away his secret.

I mention this because there is an added twist to the ZKP aspects.

You might have a Prover that is genuine (let me use the letter G to mean being genuine), which I'll call P-G for ease of reference. You might also have a Verifier that is genuine, which we'll call as V-G. But we might have spies, adversaries are what they are usually called in ZKP research, which I'll label with the letter "A" for adversarial and thus we could have a P-A (a Prover that's an adversary) and we could have a V-A that's a Verifier that's an adversary.

To be clear, we have four instances, two types of a Prover and two types of a Verifier:
- P-G: Prover Genuine
- V-G: Verifier Genuine
- P-A: Prover Adversary (spy)
- V-A: Verifier Adversary (spy)

Let's make the safest assumption about things, namely that a genuine Prover does not necessarily know that the Verifier is genuine, and nor does the genuine Verifier know that the Prover is genuine. A spy, or adversary, might be standing in place and trying to act like they are genuine. One never knows.

Thus, we have these four circumstances when an event occurs:

- P-G parlays with V-G (this is the usual expected parlay)

- P-G parlays with V-A (the Verifier is an adversary, a spy in our midst)

- P-A parlays with V-G (the Prover is an adversary, trying to trick a genuine Verifier)

- P-A parlays with V-A (it's classic spy-versus-spy, though neither might realize it!)

These circumstances are important because the Prover should be cautious about revealing anything about the secret when trying to prove the veracity of the claim about the Prover knowing the secret, since otherwise they might be revealing something to an adversary (a spy!), the no-good evil V-A. Don't want to do that. Lindt got so riled-up about the American scientist's lousy formula that Lindt revealed entirely the missing piece, the one thing that the American scientist had been seeking all along and had endured his false defection to obtain.

Generally, with ZKP, you want to avoid having to pre-establish trust between the Prover and the Verifier, if you can avoid it (this is considered a trustless setup, meaning they don't need to particularly trust each other per se, which reduces other potential burdens). If feasible, the Prover and Verifier should be able to come upon each other, transact their business, and yet feel relatively safe that the Prover did not give away something, and they were in essence complete strangers when they came together. If they have to be trusted buddies beforehand to make things work, it's going to create potential holes in the robustness and make the scheme more arduous to employ (you can do it that way, I'm just saying it is perhaps less parsimonious).

I'll make things even harder.

Let's assume that you have an observer, O, which might be one or more others that are watching the Prover and the Verifier. The observers might be prying adversaries, spies, bent on finding out the secret that the Prover possesses. Once again, the Prover is not supposed to reveal the secret, and nor any clues about it, such that then any adversarial observers are still in-the-dark about the secret itself.

Consider too the Verifier. The Verifier might know the secret already, and they are merely trying to find out whether the Prover knows it too, such as if my pal at the computer center had already known the PIN, he might have wanted to discover whether I really know it too. In fact, it just so happened that he did not know the PIN, and it was only me that knew it. The point is that the Verifier can be in one of two conditions, they know the secret, or they do not know the secret.

This is worthy of consideration since sometimes people get confused about ZKP and assume that both parties, the Prover and the Verifier, both know the secret. This does not need to be the case. My pal did not know the PIN. He was solely interested in knowing whether I knew the PIN. I'm sure he would have gladly wished that I might have divulged the PIN, either accidentally or intentionally, but that would have gotten me into great trouble.

REVEALING YOUR HAND

This brings me to my second movie that is a favorite spy story and ties to ZKP.

Sean Connery, usually known as James Bond, the infamous "spy" (a good guy spy), appeared in the movie *The Russia House*, playing the character Barley Scott-Blair, a has-been British book publisher, and a normal person that has no particular special skills or powers. He routinely visits Moscow for business purposes.

He meets a beautiful and low-key Soviet woman, Katya Orlova, played by actress Michelle Pfeiffer, and SPOILER ALERT, they fall for each other (spying and romance, once again!), somewhat at her doing, since she is trying to connect a character known as "Dante" (superbly played by actor Klaus Brandauer), which is not his real name and he is hiding his identify, but for which Katya knows, with Barley.

It turns out that Dante is a top Soviet physicist and he has a manuscript that details nuclear arms secrets, which he wants to reveal to the British and the Americans in hopes of staving off an all-out nuclear war. But the CIA and MI6 are dubious that Dante is really a top Soviet physicist. So, the CIA and MI6 concoct a list of questions for this Dante and ask Barley (Sean Connery) to meet privately with Dante and have Dante answer the questions.

Sounds good. A private meeting between Dante, the alleged Soviet physicist that wants to do "the right thing" and share Soviet nuclear secrets with the Americans and the British, via the British book publisher. Keep in mind that Barley, the British book publisher, knows nothing at all about nuclear arms. He will merely collect the answers from Dante and bring them back to the CIA and MI6, so that nuclear experts there can ascertain whether Dante knows what he claims to know.

Are you ready for the connection to ZKP?

Once the CIA and MI6 give the questions to Barley, and Barley goes to meet with Dante, it suddenly dawns on the CIA and MI6 that maybe they've just shot their own foot. How? They realize that the list of questions is a kind of reveal. The questions themselves showcase aspects about nuclear arms in a manner that inadvertently suggests what the Americans and British know about nuclear arms. Ouch!

The mere act of asking questions can be a tell.

Suppose you have planned a surprise birthday party for a friend of yours. Nobody leaks the secret. The day before the event, you see your friend, and you ask them pointedly what they are doing tomorrow at noon. Your friend, not having previously suspected that a surprise birthday party might be planned, gets highly suspicious that you would ask such a question. You have revealed a clue about a secret.

When you have a Prover that is trying to prove the veracity of a claim of a secret, I've emphasized that the Prover is not to reveal the secret and nor any clues about it. You might have a Verifier that rather than merely receiving your proof, might instead be asking a question or series of questions, doing so to essentially manufacture the proof by the answers that you provide. If so, the Verifier has to be mindful of not asking questions that could either reveal the secret and nor any clues about the secret, assuming that the Verifier knows what the secret is (as learned from *The Russia House* movie!).

In ZKP, there are interactive proof-of-knowledge processes and there are non-interactive proof-of-knowledge processes. As you can likely see, the interactive approach has the potential for either the Prover leaking the something, or for the Verifier leaking the something. They both need to be quite careful in what they say or do. You don't want happenstance of loose lips to sink the ship.

This brings up another variant that sometimes is considered. Should you consider using potential falsehoods or extraneous elements in your proof-of-knowledge to possibly throw-off an adversary that is playing the role of a Prover or Verifier, or to throw-off any observers (spies) that are watching the matter?

Putting on your spy hat, think of the clue's aspects of ZKP in terms of a set of clues, which I'll call C. So far, I've emphasized that the set C is supposed to be the null set, namely there aren't any clues provided. That's the conventional wisdom, and likely the more facile way to go.

There might though be a tradeoff involving reducing computational expense or time-effort if you are willing to reveal some clues in the course of displaying the proof (or, as I'll mention in a moment, maybe raise the bar on your adversaries).

I might be willing to showcase some genuine clues, refer to them as C-G, depending upon the payoff involved in doing so. Meanwhile, I might also be willing to offer some false clues, which I'll refer to as adversarial clues, C-A, doing so to distract or confound any adversaries that might be immersed in the matter.

I could have a set C that has only C-A members, meaning it is entirely fake clues, or I might have a set C that has only C-G members, meaning all bona fide clues, or I might have a mixture of both C-G and C-A, doing so to potentially hide the genuine ones, the C-G's, among the fake ones, C-A's. This set will be ascertained for any particular instance of a Prover and Verifier encounter.

Notice that the use of clues is going to hopefully make life harder for any adversaries, since they are now needing to contend with clues, for which they aren't sure which are genuine, and which are not. That's handy. The downside potentially is that the clues might undermine the efforts of a P-G parlaying with a V-G, making it more arduous for them to achieve their goals. Again, it's a balance of the need to make life hard for adversaries, and still get to the desired proof-of-knowledge.

Some would say this is heresy since the core principle is "zero knowledge" revealed, and the use of clues would potentially undercut that notion, though if the clues are all C-A, you could claim that it is still a zero knowledge reveal in terms of not having revealed any genuine facets.

I presumably would only reveal any minimal C-G's, if any at all, and so you might say this is a "zero-min knowledge" threshold (that's my own verbiage, not a standard), meaning that I might provide zero knowledge or some minimal amount of knowledge, doing so as a variant of trying to confound adversaries and also if it might provide some other worthy payoff such as reductions in computational expense or time.

USING SUBTERFUGE AS AN EXPLOIT

Let's ponder the potential of falsehoods or extraneous and potentially misleading elements.

My manager at the computer center had gotten her degree at another university, a college considered a rival of the university she now worked at and that I was attending. In her office, she had banners of the rival college, but none of the one that was now providing her a weekly paycheck. Strange perhaps, but true.

Suppose my pal, while trying to get me to verify that I had the PIN to the manager's office, asked me to go back into the office and wave a banner of our college. If he asked me to do so, I would be highly suspicious of him, since I knew that there wasn't such a thing in her office. Upon his asking me to show a banner, if I said yes, it would make him suspicious of me that I apparently thought there was a banner in there, which would certainly be implied by his having asked me to show one.

The banner has nothing to do with the PIN in terms of showcasing the PIN or providing any clue about the PIN. It has to do with me, the Prover, and him, the Verifier, trying to sound out each other and ascertaining whether one of us, or maybe both, are really spies and don't know the secret PIN at all.

This can though lead us down a bit of a rabbit hole. Did the Verifier ask a question that was by-design trying to determine my veracity, or did they accidentally ask a mistaken question, or were they the spy and didn't realize that the question was a potential reveal?

This brings up a related matter. If an observer were watching me and my pal, and they watched as I disappeared, and they saw the light go on and off, and the blinds getting flipped, what would they now know? They still do not know the PIN, and nor have any clues about the PIN.

You might say though that the observers do know that I apparently have the PIN, which in of itself might be a bad thing for them to be able to ascertain. Imagine if other student-workers in the computer center were watching me and my pal, they could now potentially confront me and claim that they believe I have the PIN, maybe asking me to grab some spare keyboards and printer cartridges from the manager's office.

There is a chance though that me and my pal had actually colluded all along, neither of us having the PIN. Maybe beforehand, we prearranged to have a timer or switch on the lights, and we had a contraption that would flip the blinds. The whole demonstration might be a ruse. We could simply tell the other student-workers that challenged us that we did the whole thing as an April Fool's prank, and they would not have any means per se to disprove the claim.

THE ROLE OF CERTAINTY AND PROBABILITIES

Recall that I had earlier stated that upon turning the light on and off, my pal was somewhat convinced that I had the PIN, but he was not entirely convinced. I offered to make a second visit, which then added to his level of confidence that I likely did have the PIN. I might have done a similar act a third time, a fourth time, and so on, and in so doing the odds that I really did have the PIN would seemingly continue to increase, assuming that I was each time able to do something that showcased the likelihood that I did have the PIN.

Typically, with ZKP, the Prover is demonstrating that they likely know the secret and yet it is not necessarily to a one-hundred percent degree certainty that the Prover does know the secret. The Verifier has to decide what degree of certainty or probability they are willing to accept as sufficient for the proof-of-knowledge. For my pal, the apparent fact that I had seemingly turned the lights on and off, well, it alone would or could have been sufficient proof that I have the PIN.

The Verifier though might want to be more assured about the chances of the Prover really possessing the secret. If you can setup a set of challenges, doing so in a savvy statistical way, it allows the certainty to be so high, assuming the Prover attains the challenges, you can be relatively assured that the Prover does have the knowledge claimed. You might still have a bit of nagging doubt, but it is hopefully so small that you are willing to absorb it and not feel you are taking an excessive risk at believing the claim.

In that sense, Zero Knowledge Proofs are probabilistic verification. There are some that say they don't want to use something that provides any chance of risk or uncertainty. Not even if the risk is infinitesimal. For them, a one-in-a-zillion chance that you are perhaps falsely accepting the proof-of-knowledge is too much for them. The usual retort is that they likely already are absorbing risk that they don't even realize they are, and they are blind to the risk and uncertainties of things that do have uncertainty and yet they are unaware that they do.

Remember, the only "certain" things in life are death and taxes.

WAYS TO EXPLAIN ZKP

There are several instructive stories or tales that are often used to explain the nature of ZKP.

One of the classic ones involves the fictional variant of the folk story of Ali Baba, used in a paper published in 1998 and entitled "How to Explain Zero-Knowledge Protocols to Your Children" (see the paper at http://pages.cs.wisc.edu/~mkowalcz/628.pdf).

The Ali Baba version for ZKP has evolved over time. I'll give you a quick recap as illustrative further about the nature of ZKP.
Imagine a cave that is a circular tunnel, consisting of one entrance, and from that entrance you can take a path to the right or a path to the left, all of which leads you back to the entrance. In the middle of the circular tunnel, we'll put a door. It's an impressive door. There is no means to open the door, unless you know the secret phrase. Okay, you twisted my arm, it's the phrase "Open Sesame" (SPOILER ALERT!).

Anyway, we have Peggy (remember, she's our Prover), and we have Victor (he's our Verifier), and Peggy knows the secret phrase, but Victor does not. Please do not reveal the secret phrase since I'll get in trouble with Peggy, thanks. Victor wants to have Peggy prove or provide proof-of-knowledge about the secret phrase that opens the door, meanwhile Peggy does not want to reveal what the phrase is (she's a zero-knowledge non-revealer). This should seem familiar as a setup by now.

Here's what they do. Peggy goes to the entrance, steps inside, and unseen by anyone else, she chooses either the path to the right or the path to the left. Victor then comes up to the entrance. He stands just inside and yells out the word "right" or the word "left" which means he wants Peggy to come to the entrance from that respective side (as based on facing the tunnel entrance).

Peggy indeed complies and let's say Victor yelled out "left" and she shows up from that side of the tunnel. Did she do so because she happened to have gone to the left, but got stuck at the door, and waited until she heard Victor yell, or did she perhaps go to the right and had to use the secret phrase to open the door and come along to the entrance via the path on the left?

You don't know for sure which way she did it, but if she did come out to the left, you are at least at a 50/50 chance. Victor steps out of the entrance. Peggy once again picks a choice of either right or left, whichever suits her fancy. Victor steps in. He yells out say "right" again. Peggy comes out via the right side. If she can keep succeeding, you eventually are going to be statistically pretty certain that she must be using the door and she must therefore know the secret phrase (assuming that there aren't ways to cheat, like having a superpower of being able to walk through magical locked doors).

That's a handy example of ZKP.

For those of you into complexity theory and computer science, you likely know about the famous 3-color graphs problem. Whether you happen to know the 3-color problem or not, you might enjoy the online interactive demonstrator that MIT has setup, allowing you to learn about ZKP by playing a game as a Verifier and using a 3-color graph (it's easy to play and, most importantly, there isn't any homework, nor grades assigned, nor any mandatory final exam), here's the link: http://web.mit.edu/~ezyang/Public/graph/svg.html.

A handy paper on ZKP that provides mathematical formulations that you might find of interest is this one: https://www.cs.princeton.edu/courses/archive/fall07/cos433/l ec15.pdf The author, Boaz Barak, uses a Coke versus Pepsi challenge, now a popular ZKP example, as illustration.

Essentially, you claim as the Prover that you can tell the difference between Coke and Pepsi. As the Verifier, I have Coke in a paper cup in one hand, and Pepsi in a paper cup in my other hand, I put them behind my back, I might switch the cups from one to the other hand, I present you with the cup, you take a sip, and you tell me whether you have just drank Coke or Pepsi. I know which one I've given you to taste. We do these enough times, until ultimately, I either believe you or not (again, the statistical matter comes to play, akin to Ali Baba).

Rather than using the Coke versus Pepsi challenge, some like to use an example of presenting you with two balls, one let's say is red in color, the other is blue in color, and there is nothing else to distinguish one ball from the other. Maybe I'm color blind and both balls look the same to me. You inform me that you are not color blind and can discern which ball is which. I doubt you. I show you the balls, put them behind my back, maybe switch them or not, and I present the two balls, asking you to say which is red or which is blue. We do these enough times, until I believe you are in fact not color blind.

Back to the Coke versus Pepsi challenge, Barak provides two essentials about ZKP that I've somewhat implied, one about the soundness and the other about completeness, though I didn't yet formally tell you about those important criteria, he says (see page 2 of his paper):

"A proof system is sound if you can never derive false statements using it. Soundness is a minimal condition, in the sense that unsound proof systems are not very interesting."

"A proof system is complete if you can prove all true statements using it. Similarly, we say it is complete for a family L of true statements, if you can prove all statements in L using it."

One aspect to keep in mind is that there is not just one way to do Zero Knowledge Proofs. This means that somebody might approach you and say they have a means of achieving ZKP, but you should be cautious in assuming they really do. You would want to know how they came upon their approach, and as a minimum you would ask:

- Is it sound or does it exhibit soundness to a sufficient degree?

- Is it complete or does it exhibit completeness to a sufficient degree?

- Is it truly zero-knowledge in that it reveals nothing about the core knowledge at hand and nor any clues, whether overt, subtle, or by happenstance, about the core knowledge?

One of my favorite watchable videos on ZKP is Michael Rabin's talk for the Ada Lovelace Lecture on Computability (the lecture series is in honor of August Ada Lovelace):
https://www.youtube.com/watch?v=N_LG5Hcc8mM

Rabin is a well-known mathematician and computer scientist, and received the Turing Award with Dana Scott for their paper entitled "Finite Automata and Their Decision Problems," which laid out the foundation for nondeterministic machines. It's a classic paper:https://web.archive.org/web/20160304191722/http://www.cse.chalmers.se/~coquand/AUTOMATA/rs.pdf.

In the video, Rabin uses the Where's Waldo example, which has become popular as an example of ZKP.

Essentially, as you likely know, Where's Waldo typically consists of trying to find the character Waldo on a page that has lots and lots of other characters and images, thus, he is there but "hidden" by obscurity. The ZKP version is that you take a sheet of paper, cut out a hole, just large enough to showcase Waldo, you then place the paper over the book page, making sure that the hole you've made reveals Waldo.

Assuming you do this well enough, you have not revealed the location of Waldo, which is the secret, and yet "proved" that you have the knowledge of where Waldo is.

Another popular example consists of using Sudoku, the numbers game typically involving nine of 3×3 subgrids, resulting in a 9×9 overarching grid, and a kind of mathematical puzzle requiring you to use only the digits 1 to 9 to fill-in the cells. Suppose that you are able to solve the puzzle, of which there are various ways to solve it, and want to convince someone else that you did indeed find a true solution, but you don't want to show them the solution per se. Once again, you can use ZKP to essentially prove that you likely do have a solution in-hand.

You'll be happy to know that there are lots of examples involving a myriad of mathematical puzzles, such as using Hamiltonian cycles, using discrete logs, and so on. You can take a look at the papers I've already mentioned and there is a plethora of such in-depth mathematical examples.

A practical consideration about Zero Knowledge Proofs is to consider the amount of effort or time required to undertake the proof. It's handy to be able to avoid revealing your secret, but suppose it takes a lot of back-and-forth to convince the Verifier, consuming time in doing so, along with the potential for lots of computations by either or both of the Prover and Verifier in their own respective right.

For a real-time system making use of ZKP, you'd want to be relatively confident that the time crunch does not otherwise undermine what the system needs to accomplish. I'm not saying that ZKP is a computational or time-consuming beast, only pointing out that it is an important aspect to tune when implementing ZKP, as would be the case with any kind of cryptographic approach. Likewise, you'd want to ensure that there is error detecting and mitigating features included, in case there is any disruption or difficulties encountered during the course of the proof process.

One thought is that perhaps a ZKP can be done in a one-step or one-shot manner, which would obviously cut down on the back-and-forth of a multi-step approach. This is a keen idea, though difficult or hard to do under certain situations and desired thresholds. I've mentioned in my writings that one-shot Machine Learning or Deep Learning is a hoped for aspiration, yet continues to be something outside of our grasp to-date in any generalizable way: https://www.aitrends.com/selfdrivingcars/seeking-one-shot-machine-learning-the-case-of-ai-self-driving-cars/.

Here's a classic paper that discusses one-step ZKP: http://www.wisdom.weizmann.ac.il/~/oded/PSX/oren.pdf.

Speaking of practical aspects, I've already noted that the Zero Knowledge Proof approach can be used for blockchain and cryptocurrencies, which I'd bet will gradually become a wider realization of the value that such an approach provides. To me, this is a great applied example. Blockchain and cryptocurrencies though still in an infancy stage of maturation, will likely take a while to gain the kind of acceptance and widespread use of ZKP, but inexorably it makes sense to do so.

Another practical example that I like to cite involves the use of Zero Knowledge Proofs for nuclear warhead verification. In a study done for the U.S. Department of Energy, one of the difficulties about verifying whether a nuclear warhead has been made inert or not, or the magnitude of the warhead, involves having to potentially reveal secrets about the warheads themselves.

Given the distrust between the counting parties, generally the US and Russia, there is naturally resistance to do verifications if you also need to show your secrets. Here's the study: https://www.osti.gov/servlets/purl/1127356

You'll be glad to know that it does not involve putting red and blue colored balls behind your back. Instead, it involves irradiating two or more putative warheads, using high-energy neutrons, and capturing a kind of radiation result fingerprint, consisting of the neutron transmissions and emission counts.

Doing so in a ZKP manner appears to keep secret the design of the nuclear warhead and the composition of the warhead hidden and therefore avoids the touchy sticking point about such verifications. The approach could be used for deployed nuclear arms and for non-deployed ones.

Throughout these examples, the manifestation of the proof is typically:

- The Prover takes some action that showcases they likely know the secret (such as my turning the lights on and off in the office managers office, or Peggy showing up at the correct path in Ali Baba when called by Victor, or showing Waldo), yet does not reveal the secret itself (I didn't reveal the PIN, Peggy didn't reveal "Open Sesame," and Waldo's location is not revealed).

- The Prover calculates something, reveals the calculated result, suggesting they likely know the secret (as done for mathematical puzzles and the like), yet the calculated result does not reveal the secret and no clues about the secret. This is the cornerstone of computer-based ZKP.

Some in the ZKP arena have explored whether you might relax some of these characteristics, and if so, what implications arise due to the relaxation. For example, suppose you sternly cling to not revealing the secret itself, but are willing to providing clues about the secret (as per my earlier discussion herein), perhaps doing so in a manner that the clues are quite difficult for others to discern or exploit. These are variants worthy of exploration as to strengths versus weaknesses of a desired approach to ZKP.

AI SYSTEMS AND ZKP

Now that you are up-to-speed about ZKP, let's consider how this applies to AI systems.

At the Cybernetic AI Self-Driving Car Institute, we are developing AI software for self-driving cars. There are some interesting potential applications of ZKP in the AI autonomous vehicles space, which touch upon various AI elements overall, and for which we are currently exploring.

Allow me to elaborate.

I'd like to first clarify and introduce the notion that there are varying levels of AI self-driving cars. The topmost level is considered Level 5. A Level 5 self-driving car is one that is being driven by the AI and there is no human driver involved. For the design of Level 5 self-driving cars, the auto makers are even removing the gas pedal, brake pedal, and steering wheel, since those are contraptions used by human drivers. The Level 5 self-driving car is not being driven by a human and nor is there an expectation that a human driver will be present in the self-driving car. It's all on the shoulders of the AI to drive the car.

For self-driving cars less than a Level 5, there must be a human driver present in the car. The human driver is currently considered the responsible party for the acts of the car. The AI and the human driver are co-sharing the driving task. In spite of this co-sharing, the human is supposed to remain fully immersed into the driving task and be ready at all times to perform the driving task. I've repeatedly warned about the dangers of this co-sharing arrangement and predicted it will produce many untoward results.

Let's focus herein on the true Level 5 self-driving car. Much of the comments apply to the less than Level 5 self-driving cars too, but the fully autonomous AI self-driving car will receive the most attention in this discussion.

Here's the usual steps involved in the AI driving task:

- Sensor data collection and interpretation
- Sensor fusion
- Virtual world model updating
- AI action planning
- Car controls command issuance

Another key aspect of AI self-driving cars is that they will be driving on our roadways in the midst of human driven cars too. There are some pundits of AI self-driving cars that continually refer to a utopian world in which there are only AI self-driving cars on the public roads. Currently there are about 250+ million conventional cars in the United States alone, and those cars are not going to magically disappear or become true Level 5 AI self-driving cars overnight.

Indeed, the use of human driven cars will last for many years, likely many decades, and the advent of AI self-driving cars will occur while there are still human driven cars on the roads. This is a crucial point since this means that the AI of self-driving cars needs to be able to contend with not just other AI self-driving cars, but also contend with human driven cars. It is easy to envision a simplistic and rather unrealistic world in which all AI self-driving cars are politely interacting with each other and being civil about roadway interactions. That's not what is going to be happening for the foreseeable future. AI self-driving cars and human driven cars will need to be able to cope with each other.

Returning to the topic of Zero Knowledge Proofs, let's explore some areas that ZKP can be applicable to AI self-driving cars.

GAUGING WHEN ZKP COMES TO PLAY

As a rule-of-thumb, when exploring opportunities for the application of ZKP, you should consider as part of your an that you are most likely seeking a situation involving two parties (or possibly more) that want to or need to confer with each other and do so without revealing a something of interest to both parties, yet allow the parties to be comfortable that the something is known to (at least) one and believed by the other (or proven) that it is known by the one (or more).

In a straightforward manner of speaking, if you have a potential Prover and a potential Verifier, and you are concerned about what is communicated between the two, namely you don't want any secret traffic that might get broken into, you should be thinking about ZKP. It is not axiomatic that you would always choose ZKP in such a situation, but it certainly is a tool you should have in your toolkit. If it's the only tool you have, that's probably not good, since as they say, when you only have a hammer, the whole world looks like a nail.

A savvy computer scientist has an entire bag full of tricks, or tools, upon which the appropriate tool should be considered for the appropriate circumstance. If you don't yet have ZKP in your toolkit, you ought to bone-up and make sure it is included.

If you are developing an AI system involving situations of two (or more) parties carrying on a transaction of some kind, and you are at first tempted to have them exchange a password or some means of establishing trust, you might want to rethink the matter and ponder whether ZKP might be a handy option.

I'll also mention that there is not anything mutually exclusive about using ZKP and also using a more secret-based exchange-style cryptographic method, since sometimes the more the merrier. A cybersecurity mantra is to normally have multiple layers of security, similar to how your house might have locks on the doors (one layer), be in a gated community (another layer), and you have a guard dog that barks at strangers (a scary sounding all-powerful dachshund in the house).

LANDSCAPE OF POSSIBILITIES

In the case of AI self-driving cars, I'll outline some key circumstances that fit the notion of having a Prover and a Verifier, of which they might want to preserve privacy about some aspects of the matter at-hand that causes them to communicate with each other.

They are:

- V2V (vehicle-to-vehicle) electronic communication, say car to car

- V2I (vehicle-to-infrastructure) electronic communication, say car to roadway infrastructure

- V2P (vehicle-to-pedestrian) electronic communication, say car to pedestrian

- OTA (over-the-air) electronic communications, say car to auto maker cloud

- GPS (global positioning system) electronic communications, say car to GPS cloud

- In-Car NLP (natural language processing), human to car interaction

In each of these above use cases, there is a potential Prover and a potential Verifier, and they want to have some kind of discourse with each other.

For example, there is a notion that AI self-driving cars will possibly communicate electronically with pedestrians, V2P, and could include the AI sending out a message warning a pedestrian that the self-driving car is about to take the corner ahead and perhaps step back from the curb, or it might involve the pedestrian sending a message to the AI self-driving car stating that they are urgently needing to cross the street and want to jaywalk because of an emergency.

One ongoing debate involves whether or not the AI self-driving car should be emitting some kind of identification when it undertakes these electronic communications. It could be the VIN (Vehicle Identification Number) or some other kind of presumably uniquely assigned number. You might say that it makes sense for the AI self-driving car to identify itself, rather than being anonymous.

Privacy though is a serious concern and AI self-driving cars have a doozy of a privacy matter. If your AI self-driving car is continually transmitting messages with other cars (V2V), and with the roadway such as traffic signals and bridges (V2I), and with pedestrians (V2P), or any variant thereof (referred to as V2X), you are effectively leaving a trail of where your AI self-driving car has been, assuming that each such message is accompanied by an identifier of the AI self-driving car.

Would you want to go riding in your AI self-driving car and find out later on that someone could reconstruct your trip? Spooky. As such, each of these AI self-driving car messaging matters could potentially make use of ZKP.

You might be thinking that you can just strip out any identifier and send such messages, and thus there appears at first glance to be little need to do ZKP. The problem though is that imagine if someone untoward decides to send out V2V, V2I, V2P, etc., and yet they are not sincere about it, they are playing tricks on other cars, on the roadway, and on pedestrians. You want the parties to indicate they have a genuine stake in their messaging, requiring a type of verification, and prefer to do so without also conveying private info such as an identifier.

That's where ZKP can come to the rescue.

In a somewhat similar manner, consider the situation of your AI self-driving car using a GPS system to navigate around town. Assume that there is a GPS system in the cloud that your self-driving car is using. When your self-driving car asks the GPS system for the path to your destination, the reveal tells the GPS system where you are going. Once again, this is a potential privacy invasion.

I realize you might suggest that the self-driving car should merely download the GPS info, whole hog, and therefore there is no need to tattle on the location of where you are and where you are going. This though presents other problems, including the need to have sufficient memory on-board the car, plus this suggests you might not get needed real-time updates about road conditions, etc.

There is quite interesting work going on about GPS and preserving your privacy.

One such notable paper is entitled "Privacy-Preserving Shortest Path Computation" by David Wu, Joe Zimmerman, Jeremy Planul, and John Mitchell, see: https://arxiv.org/pdf/1601.02281.pdfThe focus in their research is mainly about using compression techniques for next-hop routing matrices, but the potential for using ZKP is also a consideration.

Touching more so on ZKP in this domain, the papers of "Privacy and Integrity Considerations in Hyperconnected Autonomous Vehicles" (http://www.fkerschbaum.org/pieee18.pdf), and "Plug-in Privacy for Smart Metering Billing" (https://www.fkerschbaum.org/pets11.pdf) are of keen relevance.

For more overall work on Location-Based Services (LBS) and privacy, including Mutually Obfuscating Paths (MOP), and ZKP, see the paper entitled "Preserving Location Privacy of Connected Vehicles With Highly Accurate Location Updates" (https://www.researchgate.net/publication/311549622_Preserving_Location_Privacy_of_Connected_Vehicles_With_Highly_Accurate_Location_Updates).

Some have proposed that blockchain ought to be used for many of these communications between AI self-driving cars and other systems, and indeed we are working on that aspect too. Similar to the earlier point about using ZKP for blockchain privacy in the cryptocurrency use case, the use of ZKP in the AI self-driving car use case of blockchain has equal applicability.

Conclusion

I hope that I've whetted your appetite that Zero Knowledge Proofs are a useful tool and something that you should aim to consider. Many software developers are somewhat mystified or confounded by what ZKP is, and I hope that I've turned the corner on that by my offering you an explanation herein, with examples, and with some references for you to further study, along with some pointers toward the use of ZKP in the AI self-driving cars realm.

You might say that I've offered you a proof of sorts, a proof about the viability of ZKP, and for which there's actually no need for me to keep the secret that it has viability, I'm willing to openly divulge that. But I won't though tell you the PIN number to the door of the office manager that I once worked for, some years ago. I'll never tell that.

CHAPTER 3

ACTIVE SHOOTER RESPONSE

AND

AI SELF-DRIVING CARS

CHAPTER 3

ACTIVE SHOOTER RESPONSE AND AI SELF-DRIVING CARS

Thank goodness for a heroic bus driver in Seattle. Things went haywire on an otherwise normal day (this is a real story that happened on March 27, 2019). The metro bus driver managed to save a bus of unassuming passengers from grave danger, not a danger by a wild car driver that might have veered into the bus or a large sinkhole that might have suddenly appeared in the middle of the street, but instead this involves a life-or-death matter of an active shooter menacing the streets of North Seattle.

A crazed gunman was walking around on Metro Route 75 and was wantonly firing his pistol at anything and anyone that happened to be nearby. Characterized as a senseless and random shooting spree, the active shooter took shots at whatever happened to catch his attention. Unfortunately, the bus got into his shooting sphere. The bus was on its scheduled route and unluckily came upon the scene where the gunfire was erupting.

Unsure of what was going on, the bus driver at first opted to bring the bus to a halt. The shooter decided to run up to the bus and then, shockingly, shot pointedly at the bus driver. The bullet hit the bus driver in the chest. Miraculously, he was not killed.

In spite of the injury and the intense bleeding, and with an amazingly incredible presence of mind and spirit, the bus driver took stock of the situation and decided that the right thing to do was to escape.

He could have perhaps tried to scramble out of the bus and run away, aiming to save himself and not put any thought towards the passengers on the bus. Instead, he put the bus into reverse and backed-up, which is not an easy task with a bus, and not when you are hemorrhaging from a bullet wound, and not when you have a gunman trying to kill you.

After having driven a short distance away, he then put the bus into forward drive and proceeded to get several blocks away. His effort to get the bus out of the dire situation of being in the vicinity of the meandering shooter was smart, having saved his passengers and himself from becoming clay target-like pigeons cooped up inside that bus.

Fortunately, he lived, and we can thank him for his heroics.

When asked how long it took him to decide what to do, he estimated that it all played out in maybe two seconds or so. He got shot, looked to see if he was still able to drive the bus, and figured that he could do so.

Interestingly, he had previously taken a two-day training course for bus drivers that involved how to deal with confrontations, though as you can imagine the formal course did not include dealing with a demented gunman that's taking potshots at you and your bus. That's not something covered in most bus operations classes or owner's manuals (it's more so about unruly passengers).

Taking a step back from this incident, it does seem like there has been a sad rise in the number of active shooter incidents across the United States lately. Often, the active shooter goes into a building and wreaks havoc therein.

Sometimes this occurs in a restaurant, or a nightclub, or a warehouse, or an office environment. If you are caught up in such a situation, the difficulty often involves being trapped in a confined space. The gunman has the upper hand and can just start shooting in any direction, hoping to hit those that are within the eyesight of the killing spree.

Perhaps you've taken a class on what to do about an active shooter. I've done so, which was offered for free by the building management that housed my office. The facilities team at the building decided that it might be helpful for the building occupants to know what to do when an active shooting might arise. Though I doubted that I would ever be stuck in that kind of circumstance, I figured it would be wise to take the complimentary class anyway, always wanting to be prepared.

There is a mantra that they drummed into our heads, namely run-hide-fight, or some prefer the sequence of hide-run-fight.

Those three words need to be committed to memory. You want to recall those three words when the moment of needing them is at hand. The odds are that you'll be in a state of shock when a shooting erupts, most likely feeling intense and overwhelming panic, and without memorizing the three words you might do either nothing at all or the wrong thing.

You can use variants of the three words, such as hide-flight-fight, cover-run-fight, and others, whichever is easiest for you to recall. Some even use the three words of avoid-deny-defend.

There is also some debate about the sequencing of the three words. Some believe that you should always try to hide first, and if that doesn't seem viable then run, and if that doesn't seem viable than fight. Thus, the three words are purposely sequenced in that manner.

Not everyone believes that you can always proceed in that sequence. It might be better in a given situation to run away and not consider hiding. In that case, it would be run-hide-fight as the three words to be used.

Others would say that the trouble with running is that you probably will remain momentarily as a target while undertaking the escape, while if you are hiding you are presumably or hopefully unable to get shot.

The approach selected will generally be context based. If there is no place to hide, you should not be wasting time trying to decide whether to hide or not. Time is often of the essence in these situations. Of course, those that argue for the hiding as the first step would say that you should make your decision rapidly and if the odds of hiding seem slim, resort to the escape.

The third element, the fight part, almost always is listed as the last option.

Most would say that fighting your way out of an active shooter situation should be a last resort. Unless you happen to be trained in bona fide fighting methods, and only if the fighting approach is seemingly "better" than the hide or escape methods, only then should you try to fight. Again, this is a contextual decision. The average person, if unarmed, and faced with a gunman shooting with a loaded weapon, probably does not have much chance of overtaking the shooter.

One valuable point in the class that I attended involves the notion that you can potentially get the shooter to become distracted or be perturbed off-balance by making use of the "fight" approach in even a modest way. For example, suppose you are in an office environment, you might pick-up a stapler and throw it directly at the head of the shooter. Though the stapler is unlikely to knock-out the gunman, the odds are that the shooter will flinch or duck, reflexively, generating a pause in the shooting, allowing either you or others to try and overpower the gunman or provide a short burst of time to hide or run.

I'll repeat that it all depends upon the situation. Standing up to toss a stapler might be a bad idea. It could make you into an obvious target. You will likely draw the attention of the shooter. Being in a standing position might make it easier to get shot.

Nonetheless, there might be a circumstance whereby the stapler throwing or coffee cup throwing or throwing of any object could be a helpful act.

What would you do when you are outside, and an active shooter gets underway?

You can still use the handy three words of hide-run-fight. I'll list them in that order of hide-run-fight, but please keep in mind that you might instead memorize it as run-hide-fight, whichever you so prefer. I don't want to get irate emails from readers that are upset about my somehow urging toward which of the sequences to memorize, so please memorize as you see fit.

Getting back to the matter at-hand, what would you do if you were outside and came upon an active shooter?

You would look for anything substantial that you might be able to hide behind. If there isn't anything nearby as a hideaway or if the hiding seems to be nonsensical in the moment, you would consider then whether to run. Running in an outside situation might be dicey if the shooter has a clear shot at you while you are running. When running and confined inside a building, there might be walls, pillars, and other structures that make it harder for the shooter to aim and shoot directly at you, though of course it also makes it harder for you to make a quick getaway. Being outside might not offer protective obstructions, though it might provide you with an open path to run as fast as you can.

Let's revisit the mindset of the heroic bus driver.

The bus driver wasn't standing around. He wasn't "outside" per se. He was inside a bus. At first, you might assume that being inside a bus is a pretty good form of protection. Not particularly, especially for the driver. The driver is sitting in the driver's seat, buckled in. There are glass windows all around, so that the driver can see the roadway while driving. It's kind of a sitting duck situation.

The passengers on the bus have a greater chance of dropping to the floor of the bus to hide than does the bus driver. The passengers are usually not buckled in. Plus, the design of most buses makes it hard to see into the passenger compartment area by someone standing outside that's shooting at the bus. I'm not suggesting the passengers were safe, only pointing out that overall they were likely in a less risky place of getting shot than the driver was.

One thing the passengers could not do was presumably drive the bus, at least not in the instant that the active shooter started shooting directly at the bus. I suppose if the bus driver had gotten shot badly and could not drive the bus (or died), the passengers might have tried to yank the bus driver away from the steering wheel and one of them could have tried to drive the bus. Besides the physical aspects of trying to get into the driver's seat being a barrier to this action, the question arises whether an average passenger would have known immediately how to drive the bus.

In any case, the heroic bus driver realized that he was still alive and could drive the bus. With that decision made, the next matter to ponder would have been which way to drive the bus.

Recall the three magical words, hide-run-fight.

If there was a nearby wall, maybe pull the bus behind that wall, attempting to hide the entire bus. It seems doubtful in this case that there was any nearby obstruction large enough to hide the bus behind. So, the hide approach probably wasn't viable in this situation.

This meant that the next choice would be to consider running away. Apparently, if he had chosen to drive forward, he would have been going toward the gunman. I'll assume that in the heat of the moment, the bus driver decided that going forward would make the bus a greater and easier target for the gunman. Perhaps the shooter could have raked the bus with gunfire if it proceeded to go further up the street. Or, the gunman might have had a better bead on the bus driver, possibly providing a killing shot and causing the bus to go awry.

We can also likely assume that trying to go left or right was not much of an option. The bus was probably on a normal street that would have sidewalks, houses or buildings on either side of the street, making it nearly impossible to simply make a radical left or right turn to escape. It was like being stuck inside a canyon. The sides are impassable.

Therefore, the bus driver decided to put the bus into reverse. Driving backwards is not a particularly safe action when in a bus. I'll assume he was trying to drive backwards as fast as he could. In fact, when interviewed, the bus driver said he wasn't quite sure what was behind him and hoped that there wasn't anything that he might hit. Luck seemed to overcome the unlucky moment and permitted the bus driver to rapidly back-up the bus. For more details about the matter, see this article in the Seattle Times: https://www.seattletimes.com/seattle-news/crime/one-detained-after-shooting-reported-in-north-seattle/.

You might be wondering whether the third element of the three-word approach might have been used in this situation, namely, could the bus driver have chosen to fight?

I'll dispense with the kind of fighting in which the bus driver jumps out of the bus and tries to do a hand-to-hand combat with the shooter. The bus driver was already wounded and partially incapacitated. That's enough right there to rule out this option. Even if the bus driver had not been shot, the idea of having him open the bus door, leap out, run at the shooter, well, this seems like a very low chance of overcoming the gunman and a high chance of the bus driver getting killed.

Maybe he could have tried to run over the gunman, using the bus as a weapon.

That would have been a means to "fight" the shooter. This seems to happen in movies and TV shows. I'm betting though that trying to run down a gunman that is shooting at you would not be as straightforward as the rigged efforts for making a film.

The situation seemed to be one that if the bus driver had tried to drive at the shooter, the gunman would have likely shot the bus driver dead, before the bus rammed into the shooter.

One also wonders though how hard it might be to decide to run down someone. Yes, I realize that the gunman was on a rampage and so stopping the shooting by a means of force was well-justified. If the bus driver had run down the gunman, I think we'd all have expressed that the act was appropriate in the moment. In any case, I'm guessing that the mainstay of the choice was that trying to run over the gunman was a combination of low odds of success and also a heightened risk of getting shot at further.

I'd like to add that the bus driver emphasized afterward that he was especially concerned about the bus passengers. By backing up, this would seem like a means to try and ensure greater safety for the passengers too. Consider that the bus would have been facing the gunman, thus, as the bus drove in reverse, most of the bus would be hard for the gunman to shot into. If the bus had gone forward, presumably the shooter would have had an easier time of riddling the entire bus with bullets. It could have gotten the passengers shot by random chance, even if the shooter couldn't see into the bus directly.

Let's hope that none of us ever find ourselves in such a situation. Imagine if you were the bus driver, how would you have handled things? If you were a passenger, what might you have done? These are nightmarish considerations.

Either way, I hope you will remember to hide-run-fight if you ever find yourself in such a bind.

What does this have to do with AI self-driving cars?

At the Cybernetic AI Self-Driving Car Institute, we are developing AI software for self-driving cars. One rather unusual or extraordinary edge or corner case involves what the AI should do when driving a self-driving car that has gotten itself into an active shooter setting. That's a doozy.

Allow me to elaborate.

I'd like to first clarify and introduce the notion that there are varying levels of AI self-driving cars. The topmost level is considered Level 5. A Level 5 self-driving car is one that is being driven by the AI and there is no human driver involved. For the design of Level 5 self-driving cars, the auto makers are even removing the gas pedal, brake pedal, and steering wheel, since those are contraptions used by human drivers. The Level 5 self-driving car is not being driven by a human and nor is there an expectation that a human driver will be present in the self-driving car. It's all on the shoulders of the AI to drive the car.

For self-driving cars less than a Level 5, there must be a human driver present in the car. The human driver is currently considered the responsible party for the acts of the car. The AI and the human driver are co-sharing the driving task. In spite of this co-sharing, the human is supposed to remain fully immersed into the driving task and be ready at all times to perform the driving task. I've repeatedly warned about the dangers of this co-sharing arrangement and predicted it will produce many untoward results.

Let's focus herein on the true Level 5 self-driving car. Much of the comments apply to the less than Level 5 self-driving cars too, but the fully autonomous AI self-driving car will receive the most attention in this discussion.

Here's the usual steps involved in the AI driving task:
- Sensor data collection and interpretation
- Sensor fusion
- Virtual world model updating
- AI action planning
- Car controls command issuance

Another key aspect of AI self-driving cars is that they will be driving on our roadways in the midst of human driven cars too. There are some pundits of AI self-driving cars that continually refer to a utopian world in which there are only AI self-driving cars on the public roads.

Currently there are about 250+ million conventional cars in the United States alone, and those cars are not going to magically disappear or become true Level 5 AI self-driving cars overnight.

Indeed, the use of human driven cars will last for many years, likely many decades, and the advent of AI self-driving cars will occur while there are still human driven cars on the roads. This is a crucial point since this means that the AI of self-driving cars needs to be able to contend with not just other AI self-driving cars, but also contend with human driven cars. It is easy to envision a simplistic and rather unrealistic world in which all AI self-driving cars are politely interacting with each other and being civil about roadway interactions. That's not what is going to be happening for the foreseeable future. AI self-driving cars and human driven cars will need to be able to cope with each other.

Returning to the topic of what the AI should do when encountering an active shooter, let's consider the various possibilities involved.

I'll readily concede that the odds of an AI self-driving car coming upon a scene that involves an active shooter is indeed an edge or corner case. An edge or corner case is considered a type of situation or part of a problem that can be dealt with later on when trying to solve an overarching problem. You focus on the core parts first, and then gradually aim to deal with the edges or corner cases. For AI self-driving cars, the core or primary focus right now is getting the AI to be able to safety drive a car down a normal street on a normal day. That's a handful right there.

For the active shooter aspect, I am okay with saying it is an edge case. Hopefully there won't be many of those instances.

There are some AI developers that might say that not only is it an edge case, it is a far-off edge case. It is maximum edge. They would suggest that there really isn't much that can be done on the matter anyway. So, besides the same odds as worrying that the AI self-driving car might get struck by a falling meteor, those AI developers would say that the AI wouldn't be able to do much about the situation and thus toss the matter into the not-gonna-work-on-it bin.

I'm not so willing to concede that there isn't anything the AI can do about an active shooter situation.

For the moment, let's set aside the low odds of it happening. We'll focus instead on what to do – in the extraordinary case, if the astronomically low odds happen to befall an unlucky AI self-driving car and it comes upon an active shooter.

Also, I'm going to focus herein only on the true Level 5 AI self-driving car, one in which the AI is solely doing the driving and there isn't any co-sharing with a human driver. If the AI is co-sharing the driving, I'm assuming that by-and-large the human would take over the driving controls and try to deal with the situation, rather than the AI having to do so on its own.

Begin by considering what the AI might do if it was not otherwise developed to cope with the situation. Thus, this is what might happen if we don't give due attention to this edge case and allow the "normal" AI that's been developed for the core aspects of driving to deal with the situation at-hand.

First, the question arises about detection. Would the sensors of the self-driving car detect that there was an active shooter? Probably not, though let's clarify that aspect.

The odds are that the sensors would indeed detect a "pedestrian" that was near or on the street. The AI system would be unlikely though to ascribe a hostile intent to the pedestrian, at least not more so than any instance of a pedestrian that might be advancing toward the self-driving car. The gunman won't necessarily be running at the self-driving car as though he is desiring to ram into it. That's something that the AI could detect, namely a pedestrian attempting to physically attack or run into the self-driving car.

I'd guess that the gunman is more likely to let his gun do the talking, rather than necessarily charging at the self-driving car on foot.

If the gunman is standing off to the side and shooting, the normally programmed AI for a self-driving car won't grasp the concept that the person has a gun, and that the gun is aimed at the self-driving car, and that the gunman is shooting, and that there are lethal bullets flying, and that those bullets are hitting the self-driving car. None of that would be in the normal repertoire of the AI system for a self-driving car.

That kind of logical thinking is something that AI does not yet have per se. There isn't any kind of everyday common-sense reasoning for AI as yet. Without common sense reasoning, the AI is not going to be driving a car in the same manner that a human driver would. A human driver would likely be able to make sense of the situation. They would discern what is happening. It might be surprising, it might be unnerving, but at least the human would comprehend the notion that an active shooter was on the attack.

The AI then is not going to do anything special about there being an active shooter. In the bus driver scenario, it's likely the AI would have just kept driving forward. Unless the shooter ran into the street and stood directly in front of the AI self-driving car, there would be no reason for the AI to stop the self-driving car or consider going into reverse. The shooter presumably could have just kept shooting into the self-driving car.

If there weren't any occupants inside the AI self-driving car, the worse that would happen is that the shooter might disable the self-driving car. That's not good, but at least no human would be injured. Though, if the bullets hit inside the self-driving car in just the wrong way, it is conceivable that the AI self-driving car might go wayward, perhaps inadvertently hitting someone that might be a bystander.

If there was an occupant or various passengers in the self-driving car, the situation might make them into sitting ducks. The AI self-driving car would not realize that something is amiss. It would be driving the legal speed limit or less so, trying to drive safely down the street.

The passengers would need to either persuade the AI to drive differently, or they might need to hide inside the self-driving car and hope the bullets don't hit them, or they might need to escape from the AI self-driving car.

For the escape from an AI self-driving car, the occupants might try to tell the AI to slow down or come to a stop, allowing them to leap out. If the AI won't comply, or if it takes too long to do so, the occupants might opt to get out anyway, even while the self-driving car is in-motion. Of course, jumping out of a moving car is not usually a wise thing to do, but if it means that you can avoid possibly getting shot, it probably would be a worthy risk.

Suppose the occupants try to tell the AI what is happening and do so to persuade the AI to drive the self-driving car in a particular manner, differently than just cruising normally down the street. This is not going to be easy to have the AI "understand" and once again brings us into the realm of common sense reasoning (or the lack thereof).

You could try to make things "easy" for the AI by having the human occupants merely tell the AI to stop going forward and immediately go into reverse, proceeding to back-up as fast as possible. This seems at first glance like a simple way to solve the matter. But let's think about this. Suppose there wasn't an active shooter. Suppose someone that was in an AI self-driving car instructed the AI to suddenly go in reverse and back-up at a fast rate of speed.

Would you want the AI to comply?

Maybe yes, maybe no. It certainly is a risky driving maneuver. You could argue that the AI should comply, as long as it can do so without hitting anything or anybody. This raises a thorny topic of what kind of commands or instructions do we want to allow humans to utter to AI self-driving cars and whether those directives should or should not be obediently and without hesitation carried out by the AI.

It's a conundrum.

I'll challenge you with an even tougher conundrum. We've discussed so far that there is the hide-run-fight as a means to respond to an active shooter. The bus driver selected to run in this case. We've ruled out that hiding seemed a possibility. We then have leftover the "fight" option.

For an AI self-driving car, suppose there are human occupants, and they are in the self-driving car when it encounters an active shooter setting. I've just mentioned the idea that the humans might instruct the AI to escape or run away from the situation.

Imagine instead if the human occupants told the AI to "fight" and proceed to run down the active shooter?

Similar to the discussion about the bus driver, I think we'd agree that trying to run over the active shooter would seem morally justified in this situation. Unfortunately, we are now into a very murky area about AI. If the AI has no common-sense reasoning, and it cannot discern that this is a situation of an active shooter, it would be doing whatever the human occupants tell it to do.

What if human occupants tell the AI to run someone down, even though the person is not an active shooter. Maybe the person is someone the occupants don't like. Maybe it is a completely innocent person and a randomly chosen stranger. Generally, I doubt we want the AI to be running people down.

You could invoke one of the famous Isaac Asimov's "three laws" of robotics (it's not really a law, it is just coined as such), which states that robots aren't supposed to harm humans. It's an interesting idea. It's an idealistic idea. This notion about robots not harming humans is one that has its own ongoing debate about, and I'm not going to address it further herein, other than to say that the jury is still out on the topic.

In any case, for the moment, I think we might rule-out the possibility that the AI would be instructed to run down somebody and that the AI would "mindlessly" comply.

To clarify, someone might ask the AI to do so, but I'm saying that presumably the AI has been programmed to refuse to do so (at least for now).

Here's then where things are with the current approach to AI self-driving cars and an active shooter predicament:

- The AI won't particularly detect an active shooter situation.

- The AI correspondingly won't react to an active shooter situation in the same manner that a human driver might.

- Furthermore, human occupants inside the AI self-driving car are likely to be at the mercy of the AI driving as though it is just a normal everyday driving situation. This would tend to narrow the options for the human occupants of what they might do to save themselves.

And that's why I argue that we do need to have the AI imbued with some capabilities that would be utilized in an active shooter setting. Let's consider what that might consist of.

First, it is worth mentioning that some would argue that this is yet another reason to have a remote operator that can take over the controls of an AI self-driving car. The notion being that there is a "war room" operation someplace with humans that are trained to drive a self-driving car, and when needed they are ready and able to take over the controls, doing so remotely.

This is an approach that some believe has merit, while others question how viable the notion is. Concerns include that the remote driver is reliant on whatever the sensors can report and with delays of electronic communication might be unable to truly drive the self-driving car in real-time safely. Etc.

For the moment, let's assume there is no remote human operator in the situation, either because there is not a provision for this remote activity, or the capability is untenable.

All we have then is the AI on-board the self-driving car. It alone has to be prepared for the matter.

How would the AI ascertain that an active shooter and an active shooting is underway in its midst?

The answer would seem to be found in examining how a human driver would ascertain the same matter. It is likely that the bus driver in Seattle was able to see that the gunman was in or near the street and was carrying a gun. The gunman might have appeared to be moving in an odd or suspicious manner, which might have been detected by knowing how pedestrians usually would be moving. There might have been other people nearby that were fleeing. In a manner of speaking, it is the Gestalt of the scene.

An AI system could use the cameras and other sensors to try and determine the same kinds of telltale aspects. Let's be straightforward and agree that there could be somewhat everyday circumstances that might have these same characteristics and, yet, not be an active shooting setting. This means that the AI needs to gauge the situation on the basis of probabilities and uncertainties. Not until the point at which there are actual gun shots being detected would a more definitive classification be seemingly feasible.

Once we have V2V (vehicle-to-vehicle) electronic communications as part of the fabric of AI self-driving cars, it would imply that whichever cars or other vehicles first come upon such a scene are potentially able to send out a broadcast warning to other nearby AI self-driving car to be wary. If the bus driver had gotten a heads-up before driving onto that part of the Metro Route, he undoubtedly would have taken a different path and avoided the emerging dire situation.

Albeit even if there was V2V, this doesn't necessarily provide much relief for those AI self-driving cars that would first happen upon the scene of the shooting.

If we assume that there wasn't a tip or heads-up by V2V, nor by V2I (vehicle-to-infrastructure), and nor via V2P (vehicle-to-pedestrian), those AI self-driving cars arriving at the place and time of an active shooting have to figure out on their own what is taking place.

I've already mentioned that the human passengers, if any, might be able to clue-in the AI about the situation. Such an indication by the passengers would need to be taken with a grain of salt, meaning that those passengers might be mistaken, they might be drunk, they might be pranking the AI, or a slew of other reasons might explain why the passengers could be faking or falsely stating what is taking place. The AI would presumably need to have its own means to try and double-check the passenger's claims.

Another element would be the gunshots themselves. Humans would likely realize there is a gunman shooting due to the sounds of the gun going off, even if the humans didn't see the gun or see the muzzle blast or otherwise could not visually see that a shooting was underway.

I've previously written about and spoken about the importance of AI self-driving cars being able to have audio listening capabilities outside the self-driving car, doing so if for no other purpose than detecting the sirens of emergency vehicles. Those audio listening sensors could be another means of detecting an active shooting situation when a gun goes off. I suppose too that there might be screaming and yelling by those nearby or immersed in the setting that might be other indicator of something amiss.

Detection of the active shooting is the key to then deciding what to do next.

If the AI has detected that there is an active shooting, which might be only partially substantiated and therefore just a suspicion, the AI action planning subsystem needs to be ready to plan out what to do accordingly. There's not seemingly much point in only having an ability to detect an active shooting without also making sure that the AI will alter the driving approach once the detection had been undertaken.

The point being that each of the stages of the AI self-driving car driving tasks must be established or imbued with the active shooter responsiveness capabilities.

The sensors need to be able to detect the situation. The sensor fusion needs to put together multiple clues as embodied in the multitude of sensory data being collected. The virtual world modeling subsystem has to model what the situation consists of. The AI action planner needs to interpret the situation and do what-if's with the virtual world model, trying to figure out what to do next. The plan, once figured out, needs to be conveyed via the self-driving car controls commands.

What kind of AI action plans might be considered and then undertaken?

Hide-run-fight.

That's the hallmark of what the AI needs to review. Similar perhaps to the bus driver, each of the approaches would involve trying to gauge whether the chosen action will make for greater danger or lessen the danger. In this case, the danger would be primarily about potential injury or death to the passengers of the self-driving car, though that's not the only concern. For example, suppose the AI self-driving car could make a fast getaway by driving up onto a nearby sidewalk, but in so doing it might be endangering pedestrians that are on the sidewalk and perhaps fleeing the scene on foot.

Should the AI self-driving car consider the "fight" possibilities?

As mentioned earlier, it's a tough one to include. If a "fight" posturing would imply that the AI would choose to try and runover the presumed active shooter, it opens the proverbial Pandora's box about purposely allowing or imbuing the AI with the notion of injuring or killing someone. Some critics would say that it is a slippery slope, upon which we should not get started. Once started, those critics worry how far might the AI then proceed, whether the circumstance warranted it or not.

Conclusion

I'm sure we all would hope that we'll never be drawn into an active shooter setting.

Nonetheless, if a human driver were driving a car and came upon such a situation, it's a reasonable bet that the driver would recognize what is happening, and they would try to figure out whether to hide, run, or fight, making use of their car, if they otherwise did not think that abandoning the car and going on-foot was the better option.

AI self-driving cars are not yet being setup with anything to handle these particular and admittedly peculiar situations.

That makes sense in that the focus right now is nailing down the core driving tasks. As an edge or corner case, dealing with an active shooter is a lot further down on the list of things to deal with.

In any case, ultimately there are ways to expand the AI's capabilities to try and cope with an active shooting setting. Most of what I have described could be a kind of add-on pack to an existing AI self-driving car and provide an additional capability into the core once the software for this specialty was established. It's the kind of add-on feature that an OTA (Over-the-Air) update could then be used to download the module into the on-board AI system at a later date.

In theory, maybe we will be living in a Utopian society once AI self-driving cars are truly at a Level 5 and no one will ever be confronted by an active shooter. Regrettably, I doubt that society will have changed to the degree that there won't still be instances of active shooters. For that reason, it would be wise to have an AI self-driving car that is versed in how to contend with those kinds of life-and-death moments.

CHAPTER 4

FREE WILL
AND
AI SELF-DRIVING CARS

CHAPTER 4

FREE WILL

AND

AI SELF-DRIVING CARS

Perhaps one of the oldest questions asked by humans is whether or not there is free-will. It's up there with questions such as why we all exist, how did we come to exist, and other such lofty and seemingly intractable queries. If you are anticipating that I'm going to tell you definitively herein whether there is free-will or not, I guess you'll have to keep reading, and the choice you make will determine the answer to your question.

I'll pause while you ponder my point.

Okay, let's get back underway.

Well, since you are now presumably reading these words, I gather that you choose to keep reading. Did you make that choice of your own free-will?

We generally associate free-will with the notion that you are able to act on your own, making your own decisions, and that there isn't any particular constraint on which way you might go. Things get muddy quite quickly when we begin to dig deeper into the matter.

As I dig into this, please be aware that some people get upset about how to explain the existence of or the lack of free-will, typically because they've already come to a conclusion about it, and therefore any discussion on the matter gets things pretty heated up. I'm not intending to get the world riled up herein.

As you'll see in a few moments, my aim is to layout some of the key landscape elements on the topic, and then bring it into a vantage point that will allow for considering other points I'd like to make about AI and AI systems.

Indulge me as I try to get us there.

Free-Will Or Non-Free-Will: That's The Question

If I were to suggest that the world is being controlled by a third-party that was unseen and undetected, and that we were all participants in a play being undertaken by this third party, it becomes hard to either prove that you have free-will if you claim you do, or prove that you don't have free-will.

Were you to contend that you do have free-will, you are actually saying so under a false pretense or belief, since I've claimed that you are merely part of a play, and you are unaware of the play taking place and aren't able to discern the director that is guiding the action. On the other hand, there's no evidentiary means to prove that you are not exercising free-will, since the director is unseen and the play itself is unknown to us, instead it is merely life as it seemingly unfolds.

You can make this into a combo deal by suggesting that the play is only an outline, and you still have some amount of free-will, as exercised within the confines of the play. The problem though with this viewpoint is that someone else might contend that there is either free-will or there is not free-will, and if you are ultimately still under the auspices of the play, you don't have true free-will. You have a kind of muted or constrained free-will.

For those that believe in the binary sense of free-will, meaning you either have it entirely and without any reservation and no limits, that's their version of the binary digit one, and anything else is considered a binary digit of a zero. Therefore, they would reject that you have free-will unless and only if it is utterly unfettered. No gray areas, no fuzzy logic allowed.

Set aside for the moment the third-party notion and consider another perspective.

Maybe everything that seems to be happening is already predetermined, as though it was a script and we are simply carrying out the script. We don't see the script and don't realize it is a script. We don't know how the script came to be, which of course goes along with the idea that we cannot see it and don't realize it exists.

Somehow, we are making decisions and taking actions that have been already decided. It could be that the script is extensive to the nth degree, covering every word you say, every action you take. Or, it could be a script that has preferred lines and preferred actions, yet you still can do some amount of improvisation.

Once again, proving that you are not abiding by the written script is not feasible, because there isn't proof of the script and nor that you are acting upon it. In essence, it doesn't seem likely that under this script milieu we can prove you do or do not have free-will.

Another take on the free-will underpinnings relates to cause and effect.

Perhaps everything that we do is like a link in a very long chain, each link connecting to the next. Any decision you make at this moment is actually bound by the decision that was made moments earlier, which is bound to the one before that, and so on, tracing all that you do back to some origin point. After the original origin point occurred, all else was like a set of dominos, each domino cascading down due to the one that came before it that had moments before fallen down.

The past is the past.

The future is not necessarily already written. I

t could be that this moment, right now, consists of one of those dominos, about to fall, and once it falls, the next thing that happens is as a direct and unyielding result of the falling domino that just fell. In this perspective, the future could be unplanned and open ended, though it is entirely dependent on the decisions and actions that came before.

Some would describe this viewpoint of your steps being either laid out or as being inextricably connected as depicting what might be commonly called fate, typically considered something that has been predetermined and you are in a sense merely carrying it out, an inch at a time. The word destiny is used in a somewhat similar sense, though usually suggested as a target point, rather than the steps in-between, such as it is your destiny to become rich and famous, though how you get there is perhaps not predetermined, yet you will indeed get there.

In the philosophy field, a concept known as determinism (not to be confused with the computer science meaning) is used to suggest that we are bound by this cause-and-effect aspect. You can find some wiggle room to suggest that you might still have free-will under determinism, and so there's a variant known as hard determinism that closes off that loophole and claims that dovetailing with the cause-and-effect there is no such thing as free-will.

Depending upon which philosopher you happen to meet while getting a cup of java at your local coffee bar, they might be a compatibilistic believer, meaning that both determinism and free-will can co-exist, or they might be an incompatibilistic believer, asserting that if there is determinism then there is no such thing as free-will.

Some are worried that if you deny that free-will exists, it implies that perhaps whatever we do is canned anyway, and so it apparently makes no difference to try and think things through, you could presumably act seemingly arbitrarily.

In that case, your arbitrariness is not actually arbitrary, and it is only you thinking that it is, when in fact it has nothing to do with randomness and one way or another it was already predetermined for you. Thus, chuck aside all efforts to try and decide what to do, since the decision was already rendered.

This kind of thinking tends to drive people toward a type of fatalism. At times, they can use this logic to opt to transgress against others, shrugging their shoulders and saying that it was not them per se, it was instead whatever non-free-will mechanism that they assert brought it to fruition.

Of course, under a non-free-will viewpoint, maybe those that kept trying to think things through were meant to do so, as due to the third-party or due to the script or due to the cause-and-effect, while people that shift into seemingly being purely arbitrary are actually under the spell of one of those predetermined approaches.

One additional twist is the camp that believes in free-won't.

Let's consider the free-won't aspects.

Maybe you do have some amount of free-will, as per my earlier suggestion that there could be a kind of loosey goosey version, but the manner of how it is exercised involves a veto-like capability.

Here's how that might work. You non-free-will aims to get you to wave your arm in the air, which accordingly you would undertake to do, since we're saying for the moment you don't have free-will to choose otherwise.

The free-won't viewpoint is that you do have a kind of choice, a veto choice. You could choose to not do the thing that the non-free-will stated, and therefore you might choose to not wave your arm. In this free-won't camp, note that you weren't the originator of the arm waving. You were the recipient of the arm waving command, yet you were able to exercise your own discretion and veto the command that was somehow otherwise given to you.

An important construct usually underlying this viewpoint is that you could not choose to do anything else, since that's up to the non-free-will origination aspects, and all you can do is choose to either do or not do the thing that the non-free-will commanded. Thus, your veto could be to not wave your arm, but you cannot then decide to kick your feet instead. Nope. The kicking of your feet has to originate via the non-free-will, of which then your free-won't get-out-of-jail card allows you to decide not to kick your feet, if that's what you want to choose to do.

Those that are the binary types will quickly say you obviously don't have free-will in the use case of having free-won't, in that you don't have true free-will, and you have this measly free-won't, a far cry from an unburdened free free-will. Others would say that you do have free-will, albeit maybe somewhat limited in scope and range.

I think that lays enough groundwork for moving further into the discussion overall. Do keep in mind that the aforementioned indication is just the tip of the iceberg on the topic of free-will. I've left out reams of other angles on the topic. Consult your philosophers stone for further information about free-will.

Can Free-Will Be Detected Via Neuroscience

So far, it's been suggested that for humans, we really cannot say for sure whether we have free-will or not. You can make a claim that we do have free-will, but you then have to presumably prove that there isn't this non-free-will that is over-the-top of free-will. Some say that the burden of proof needs to be on the non-free-will believers, meaning they need to showcase proof of the non-free-will, otherwise the default is that there is free-will.

Another means to try and break this logjam might be to find one "provable" instance of the existence of free-will, which at least then you could argue that free-will exists, though maybe not all the time and nor everywhere and nor with everyone.

Likewise, some say that if you could find one "provable" instance that there is the existence of non-free-will, you could argue that there is at least one case of non-free-will that presumably overpowers free-will, which might not be the case all the time or for everywhere and nor for everyone, yet it does nonetheless exist (if so proven).

This fight over free-will has drawn scrutiny by just about every domain or discipline that bears on the topic. The field of philosophy is the most obvious such domain. There is also the field of psychology, trying to unlock the mysteries of the mind, as does the field of cognitive science. We can also pile into this the neurosciences, which likewise aims to gauge how the brain works, and ultimately how the brain arrives at the act of thinking.

One key study in neuroscience that sparked quite a lot of follow-on effort was undertaken by Benjamin Libet, Curtis Gleason, Elwood Wright, and Dennis Pearl in 1983:
See https://academic.oup.com/brain/article-abstract/106/3/623/271932).

In their study, they attempted to detect cerebral activity and per their experiment claimed that there was brain effort that preceded conscious awareness of performing a physical motor-skilled act by the human subjects, as stated by the researchers:

"The recordable cerebral activity (readiness-potential, RP) that precedes a freely voluntary, fully endogenous motor act was directly compared with the reportable time (W) for appearance of the subjective experience of 'wanting' or intending to act. The onset of cerebral activity clearly preceded by at least several hundred milliseconds the reported time of conscious intention to act."

Essentially, if you were told to lift your arm, presumably the conscious areas of the brain would activate and send signals to your arm to make it move, which all seems rather straightforward. This particular research study suggested that there was more to this than meets the eye.

Apparently, there is something else that happens first, hidden elsewhere within your brain, and then you begin to perform the conscious activation steps.

You might be intrigued by the conclusion reached by the researchers:

"It is concluded that cerebral initiation of a spontaneous, freely voluntary act can begin unconsciously, that is, before there is any (at least recallable) subjective awareness that a 'decision" to act has already been initiated cerebrally. This introduces certain constraints on the potentiality for conscious initiation and control of voluntary acts."

Bottom-line, this study was used by many to suggest that we don't have free-will. It is claimed that this study shows a scientific basis for the non-free-will basis. Furthermore, the time delay between the alleged subconscious effort and the conscious effort initiation became known as Libet's W, the amount of time gap between the presumed non-free-will and the exercising of some limited kind of free-will (Libet had stated that there might be a free-won't related to the free-will portion, involving a conscious veto capability).

Not everyone sees this study in the same light. For some, it is a humongous leap of logic to go from the presumed detection of brain activity prior to other brain activity that one assumes is "conscious" activity, and then decide that the forerunner activity had anything at all to do with either non-free-will or free-will.

Many would contend that there is such a lack of understanding about the operations of the brain that making any kind of conclusion about what is happening would be treading on thin ice. There is also the qualm that these were acts involving motor skills, which are presumably going to take much long, orders of magnitude, for the enactment of, due to the physical movements, while the brain itself is able to perform zillions of mental operations in that same length of time.

Does the alleged "unconscious" related brain activity suggest that there is something afoot here, namely that it perhaps supports the theories about a omnipresent third-party that is maybe controlling the brain, or that the script theory is correct and the brain is retrieving a pre-planted script from within the recesses of your noggin, or maybe the cause-and-effect theory is validated since this shows that the "conscious" act was controlled by the "unconscious" causal effect.

And so on.

There have been numerous other related neuroscience studies, typically trying to further expound on this W and either confirm or disconfirm via related kinds of experiments. You can likely find as many opponents as proponents about whether these neuroscience studies show anything substantive about free-will.

Another qualm some have is that these are usually done as retrodiction-oriented studies, meaning that they involve examining the data after-the-fact and trying to interpret and reach conclusions thereof. Some assert that you would need to try and figure out what the brain is doing while it is actually happening, in the midst of acting, rather than recording a bunch of data and then afterward sifting through it.

For those of you are intrigued by this kind of neuroscience pursuit, you might keep your eye on the work taking place at the Institute for Interdisciplinary Brain and Behavioral Sciences at Chapman University, which has Dr. Uri Maoz as the project leader for a multi-million dollar non-federal research grant that was announced in March 2019 on the topic of conscious control of our decisions and actions as humans, with Dr. Amir Raz, professor of brain sciences and director.

Participants in the effort include Charité Berlin (Germany), Dartmouth, Duke, Florida State University, Harvard, Indiana University Bloomington, NIH, Monash University (Australia), NYU, Sigtuna (Sweden), Tel Aviv University (Israel), University College London (UK), University of Edinburgh (UK), and researchers at UCLA and Yale.

Stepwise Actions and Processes

Some would argue that the brain does not necessarily operate in a stepwise fashion and that it is raft with parallelism. Therefore, trying to lay claim that A happens before B is somewhat chancy, when in fact the odds are that A an B are actually happening at the same time or in some kind of time overlapping manner. It is perhaps more nonlinear than it is linear, and only our desire to simplify how things work involves flattening the brain operations into a step-at-a-time sequential description.

Be that as it may, let's for the moment go along with the notion of an overarching linear progression, and see where that takes us.

Consider that we have a human that is supposed to move their arm, the end result of the effort involves the arm movement, and presumably to get their arm to move there is some kind of conscious brain activity to make it happen.

We have this:

Conscious effort -> Movement of arm

According to some of the related neuroscience research, those two steps are actually preceded by an additional step, and so I need to include the otherwise hidden or unrealized step into the model we are expanding upon herein.

As such:
Unconscious effort -> Conscious effort -> Movement of arm

Let's add labels to these, as based on what some believe we can so label:
Unconscious effort (non-free-will) -> Conscious effort (free-will that's free-won't) -> Movement of arm

Here's a bit of a question for you, does the conscious effort realize that there is an unconscious effort (namely the unconscious effort that precedes the conscious effort), or is the conscious effort blissfully unaware about the unconscious effort (which presumably launched the conscious effort)?

You might say that the question relates to the earlier discussion about the knowingness or lack thereof about the non-free-will initiations. I've stated that some believe there is an undetectable third-party or a laid-out script or a cause-and-effect, none of which are seemingly knowable to us humans and therefore we can neither prove or disprove that these non-free-will controllers are acting upon us.

Maybe the conscious effort is blind to the unconscious effort, and perhaps is acting as though it is under free-will, yet it is actually not.

Or, one counter viewpoint is that maybe the conscious and unconscious work together, knowingly, and are really one overall brain mechanism and it is a fallacy on our part to try and interpret them as separate and disjointed.

Is the conscious effort a process, of its own, running on its own, or so it assumes, or might the unconscious effort and the conscious effort be running in concert with each other?

For that matter, I suppose we could even ponder whether the unconscious effort is knowingly sparking the conscious effort, which instead maybe the unconscious effort is its own independent process and it has no idea that it causes something else to happen after it acts.

I don't want to go down this rabbit hole to far, for now, and bring up what seems perhaps to be rather abstract in order to make this discussion paradoxically more concrete.

How can we make this more concrete?

Notice that I've referred to the unconscious effort and the conscious effort as each being a process.

If we shift this discussion now into a computer-based model of things, we might say that we have two processes, running on a computer, and for which they might involve one process preceding the other, or not, and they might interact with each other, or not.

These are processes happening in real-time.

It could be that either of the two processes knows about the other. Or, it could be that the two processes do not know about each other.

For anyone that designs and develops complex real-time computer-based systems, you have likely dealt with these kinds of circumstances. You have one or more processes, operating in real-time, and some of which will have an impact on the other processes, at times being in front of some other process, at other times taking place after some other process, and all of which might or might not be directly coordinated.

Consider a modern-day car that has a multitude of sensors and is trying to figure out the roadway and how to undertake the driving task.

You could have a process that involves collecting data and interpreting the data from cameras that are on the car. You might have a process that does data collection and interpretation of radar sensors. The process that deals with the cameras and the process that deals with the radar could be separate and distinct, neither one communicates with the other, neither one happens before or necessarily after the other. They operate in parallel.

AI Free-Will Question and Self-Driving Cars Too

What does this have to do with AI self-driving cars?

At the Cybernetic AI Self-Driving Car Institute, we are developing AI software for self-driving cars.

The AI system is quite complex and involves thousands of simultaneously running processes, which is important for purposes of undertaking needed activities in real-time, but also offers potential concerns about safety and inadvertent process-related mishaps.

Allow me to elaborate.

I'd like to first clarify and introduce the notion that there are varying levels of AI self-driving cars. The topmost level is considered Level 5. A Level 5 self-driving car is one that is being driven by the AI and there is no human driver involved. For the design of Level 5 self-driving cars, the auto makers are even removing the gas pedal, brake pedal, and steering wheel, since those are contraptions used by human drivers. The Level 5 self-driving car is not being driven by a human and nor is there an expectation that a human driver will be present in the self-driving car. It's all on the shoulders of the AI to drive the car.

For self-driving cars less than a Level 5, there must be a human driver present in the car. The human driver is currently considered the responsible party for the acts of the car. The AI and the human driver are co-sharing the driving task. In spite of this co-sharing, the human is supposed to remain fully immersed into the driving task and be ready at all times to perform the driving task. I've repeatedly warned about the dangers of this co-sharing arrangement and predicted it will produce many untoward results.

Let's focus herein on the true Level 5 self-driving car. Much of the comments apply to the less than Level 5 self-driving cars too, but the fully autonomous AI self-driving car will receive the most attention in this discussion.

Here's the usual steps involved in the AI driving task:
- Sensor data collection and interpretation
- Sensor fusion
- Virtual world model updating
- AI action planning
- Car controls command issuance

Another key aspect of AI self-driving cars is that they will be driving on our roadways in the midst of human driven cars too. There are some pundits of AI self-driving cars that continually refer to a utopian world in which there are only AI self-driving cars on the public roads. Currently there are about 250+ million conventional cars in the United States alone, and those cars are not going to magically disappear or become true Level 5 AI self-driving cars overnight.

Indeed, the use of human driven cars will last for many years, likely many decades, and the advent of AI self-driving cars will occur while there are still human driven cars on the roads.

This is a crucial point since this means that the AI of self-driving cars needs to be able to contend with not just other AI self-driving cars, but also contend with human driven cars. It is easy to envision a simplistic and rather unrealistic world in which all AI self-driving cars are politely interacting with each other and being civil about roadway interactions.

That's not what is going to be happening for the foreseeable future. AI self-driving cars and human driven cars will need to be able to cope with each other.

Let's return to the discussion about free-will.

AI Systems With Or Without Free-Will

Can an AI system have free-will?

This is a somewhat hotly debated topic these days. There are some that are worried that we are in the midst of creating AI systems that could become presumably sentient, and as a result, maybe they would have free-will.

You might say, great, welcome to the free-will community, assuming you believe that humans have free-will, and might believe it's a boon to the free-will population to have AI machine-based free-willers around.

On the other hand, some are suggesting that an AI that has free-will might not tow the line in terms of what we humans want the AI to be or do. It could be that the free-will AI decides it doesn't like us and using its own free-will opts to wipe us from earth or enslave us.

This would certainly seem like a rather disappointing turn of events, namely that we somehow spawned free-will into machines and they turn on us, rather than being grateful or at least respectful of us.

There are all sorts of twists and turns in that debate. If we as humans don't have free-will, presumably the creation of AI would also not have free-will, since it is being crafted by the non-free-will that forced us or led us to make such AI. Or, you could say that the non-free-will decided that it was time to allow for true free-will and figured that doing so might be wasted on humans, and as a result allowed the humans to make something that does have free-will. On and on this goes around.

I'd like to tackle at least one aspect that I believe seems to be to me be relatively clear cut.

For today's AI, tossing into it the best that anybody in AI can do right now in terms of Machine Learning and Deep Learning, along with deep Artificial Neural Networks, it would seem like this is really still a Turing Machine in action. I realize this is a kind of proof-by-reduction, in which I am saying that one thing reduces to the equivalent of another, but I think it is fair game.

Would anyone of any reasonable nature be willing to assert and genuinely believe that a Turing Machine can somehow embody or exhibit free-will?

I dare say it just seems over-the-top to think it has or could have free-will. Now, I realize that also takes us into the murky waters of what is free-will. Without getting carried away here and having to go on and on, I would shorten this to say that a Turing Machine has no such spark that we tend to believe is part of human related free-will.

I'm sure that I'll get emails right away and criticized that I've said or implied that we cannot ever have AI that might have free-will (if there is such a thing), which is not at all what I've said or implied, I believe.

For the kind of computer based systems that we use today, I believe

I'm on safe ground about this, but I quite openly say that there are future ways of computing that might well indeed go beyond what we can do today, and whether or not that might have a modicum of free-will, well, who's to say.

AI Self-Driving Cars and Lessons Based on Free-Will Debate

Let's assume that we are able to achieve Level 5 self-driving cars. If so, does that mean that AI has become sentient? The answer is not necessarily.

Some might say that the only path to a true Level 5 self-driving car involves having the AI be able to showcase common-sense reasoning. Likewise, the AI would need to have Artificial General Intelligence (AGI). If you start cobbling together those aspects and they are all indeed a necessary condition for the advent of Level 5, one supposes that the nearness to some kind of sentience is perhaps increasing.

It seems like a fairly sound bet that we can reach Level 5 without going quite that far in terms of AI advances. Albeit the AI driving won't perhaps be the same as human driving, yet it will be sufficient to perform the Level 5 driving task.

I'd like to leverage the earlier discussion herein about processes and relate that aspect to AI self-driving cars. This will give a chance to cover some practical day-to-day ground, rather than the otherwise lofty discussion so far about free-will, which was hopefully interesting, and led us to consider some everyday perfunctory matters too.

Let's start with a use case that was brought up during a recent event by Tesla that was known as their Autonomy Investor Day and involved a car and a bicycle and how the capabilities of automation might detect such aspects (the Tesla event took place on April 22, 2019 at Tesla HQ and was live-streamed on YouTube).

Use Case of The Bike On Or Off The Car

Suppose you have an AI self-driving car that is scanning the traffic ahead. Turns out that there is a car in front of the self-driving car, and this car has a bike that's sitting on a bike rack, which is attached to the rear of the car. I'm sure you've seen this many times. If you want to take your bicycle someplace, you put a bike rack onto the back of your car, and you then mount the bike onto the bike rack.

The variability of these bike racks and mountings can be somewhat surprising.

There are some bike racks that can hold several bikes at once. Some bike racks can only handle one bike, or maybe squeeze in two, and yet the person mounted say four bikes onto it. I've seen some mounted bikes that were not properly placed into the rack and looked as though they might fall out at any moment.

A friend told me that one time she saw a bike come completely off the bike rack, while a car was in-motion, which seems both frightening and fascinating to have seen. Frightening because a bike that becomes a freewheeling (ha, almost said free-will!) object on the roadway, beyond the control of a human bike rider, well, it is a scary proposition for nearby traffic and nearby pedestrians.

Imagine if you were riding your own bike in the bike lane, minding your own business, riding safely, and another bike suddenly flew off the rear of a car and smashed into you. I dare say no one would believe your story.

Suppose you were driving a car and came upon the madcap bike; it creates difficult choices.

A small dropped item like a hubcap you might be willing to simply run over, rather than making a radical and potentially dangerous driving maneuver, but a bike is a sturdier and larger object and one that by striking could do a lot of damage to the car and the bike. In a split second, you'd need to decide which was the better choice, avoid the zany bike and is so doing perhaps endanger yourself and other traffic, or ram into the bike, and possibly endangering yourself or other traffic.

Neither option is pleasant.

I did see something about a mounted bike that caught my attention one day. The bike was mounted incorrectly and protruded far beyond the rightmost side of the car. This became a dangerous kind of dagger, poking over into the lane to the right of the car. I wondered whether the driver realized what they had done, or whether they were oblivious and had not realized the predicament that had created for all other nearby car traffic.

I watched as several cars approached in the right lane, adjacent to the car with the improperly mounted bike, which was in the left lane. Those cars often seemed to fail to discern the protruding element until the last moment. Car after car would swerve suddenly to their right, attempting to avoid the spoked wheel of the bike. The swerving was not overly dangerous when there was no other traffic to the further right, but when there was other such traffic, the swerving avoiders would cause other cars in those further right lanes to also weave and semi-panic.

In any case, let's consider that there is a process in the AI system that involves trying to detect cars that are nearby to the AI self-driving car. This is typically done as a result of Machine Learning and Deep Learning, involving a deep Artificial Neural Network getting trained on the images of cars, and then using that trained capability for real-time analyses of the traffic surrounding the self-driving car.

You might have a second process that involves detecting bicycles.

Once again, it is likely the process was developed via Machine Learning and Deep Learning and consists of a deep Artificial Neural Network that was trained on images of bikes.

For the moment, assume then that we have two processes, one to find cars in the camera images and video streaming while the self-driving car is underway, and a second process to find bicycles.

During the Tesla event, an image was shown of a car with a bike mounted on a rear bike rack. It was demonstrated that the neural network automation was detecting both the car and the bike, each as independent objects.

Now, this could be disconcerting in one manner, namely if the AI is under the belief that there is a car ahead of the self-driving car, and there is also a bike ahead of the self-driving car, each of which is doing their own thing. You might be startled to think that these would be conceptually two different matters. As a human, you know that the bike is really mounted on the car and not under its own sense of motion or actions. The bike is going along for the ride, as it were.

I guess you could say that the bike has no free-will at this moment and is under the non-free-will exerted control of the car.

If the AI though is only considering the car as a separate matter, and the bike as a separate matter, it could get itself tied into a bit of a knot. The bike is facing in some particular direction, depending upon how it was mounted, so let's pretend it is mounted with the handle bars on the right-side of the car. The programming of the AI might be that it assumes a bicycle will tend to move in the direction of the handlebars, normally so.

Imagine the curious nature then of what the AI is perceiving. A car is ahead of the self-driving car. It is moving forward at some speed and distance from the self-driving car. Meanwhile, there's a bike that is just at the same distance, moving at the same speed but doing so in an oddball manner, it is moving forward yet it is facing to the side.

Where is the bike next going to be?

The standard assumption would be that the bike will be moving to the right, and thus it would be a reasonable prediction to anticipate that the bike will soon end-up to the right. If the car with the mounted bike continues straight ahead, the bike obviously won't end-up going to the right. Of course, if the car with the mounted bike were to move into the right lane, it would likely lend credence to the notion that the bike is moving and has now been bicycled into the right lane.

One viewpoint of this matter from an AI systems perspective is that the car ahead should be considered as a large blob that just so happens to have this other thing on it, but that it doesn't care what that thing is. All that is needed is to realize that the car is of a size NxM, which encompasses the added scope of the bike.

So, we have two processes, one finding cars, one finding bikes, and the bike finding process is potentially misleading the rest of the AI system by trying to clamor that there is a bike ahead of the self-driving car. The AI developers realized that this is both true and false at the same time, being that there is a bike there, but it is not a free-wheeling bike.

One reaction by the AI developers involves "fixing" the AI system to ignore a bike when it is seemingly mounted on the back of a car. There is presumably no need to detect such a bike. It doesn't matter that it so happens to be a bike. If the car had a piano mounted on the back of the car, it wouldn't matter that it was a piano, and instead merely noteworthy that the car is larger in size than might usually be the case (when you include the scope of the piano).

I certainly grasp this approach, yet it also seems somewhat worrisome.

A human knows that a bike is a bike.

A bike has wheels and it can roll around. A human knows that a bike mounted on the back of a car can come loose. A bike that comes loose can possibly fall onto the roadway like a wooden pallet, making a thud and not going anywhere, or it could potentially move more freely due to the wheels. Of course, without a bike rider, presumably the bike is not going be able to ride along per se, yet with the motion already underway as a result of being on the car, there's a chance that the bike could "roll" for some distance.

You might be objecting and saying that the odds of a bike coming off a bike rack is slim, and it would also seem slim that once the bike did fall off that it would move along on the roadway. As such, with such slim odds, it seems like a rather remote edge case and you can just reduce the whole topic to not caring about the bike, instead relying upon some other part of the AI that might deal with debris that falls onto the street.

The counter argument is that it is still worthwhile to realize that the bike is a bike, being able to therefore gauge what might happen if the bike does fall off the car. It might be best to be proactive and anticipate that such a mishap might occur, rather than waiting until it does happen and having to react, not having gotten prepared for the possibility of the mishap.

This all ties too to the topic of how much should AI systems be doing defensive driving tactics, which most are not yet doing. By-and-large, the focus by most auto makers and tech firms has been the reactive side of driving. React once something happens is the focus, rather than trying to anticipate what might happen. Novice drivers tend to be the same way.

I've emphasized many times in my writings and speeches that the lack of defensive driving tactics for the AI systems will make them brittle and vulnerable. I don't view that defensive driving as an edge or corner case to be handled at some later time, which regrettably some others do.

Conclusion

When discussing the topic of free-will, it can become quite abstract and tilt towards the theoretical and the philosophical side of things. Such discussions are worthwhile to have, and I hope that my offering of a taste of it will be of interest to you, perhaps spurring you to look further into the topic.

I've tried to also bring some of the topic to a more day-to-day realm. You can think of the free-will and non-free-will discussion as being about control or lack-of-control over processes (in a more pedantic, mundane way, perhaps).

When developing real-time AI systems, such as AI self-driving autonomous cars, you need to be clearly aware of how those processes are running and what kind of control they have, or lack thereof.

If you are the type of reader that began reading this article and upon my opening remark that maybe or maybe not that I would reveal whether humans have free-will, and if you then skipped the entire piece and jumped just to this conclusion, in hopes of seeing what I proclaimed, well, you'll have to do the hard work and actually read the whole piece.

You can then decide whether or not I did state whether free-will exists or not, doing so by your own choice of opting to actually read the piece. That's of your own free-will. Or is it?

CHAPTER 5

NO PICTURE YET
OF
AI SELF-DRIVING CARS

CHAPTER 5
NO PICTURE YET
OF
AI SELF-DRIVING CARS

Scientists were abuzz with the release of a picture depicting a supermassive black hole that is over 55 million light-years away in outer space, the first time any picture of a black hole has ever been produced, meanwhile here on Earth there is still not a picture of a true driverless car.

Yes, it is true, we do not yet have a Level 5 driverless car and no one can even say for sure what it will look like.

The efforts you keep hearing about and seeing in online videos and ads are at-most touching upon Level 4, or lesser capable levels such as Level 3 and Level 2, often improperly and inappropriately professed as self-driving or driverless cars.

Keeping Score About Driverless Cars

The official scoring system, promulgated by the Society for Automotive Engineers (SAE), indicates that a Level 5 is essentially a true driverless car, one that has the AI driving the car and there is no need for a human driver.

The Level 5 self-driving car has either passengers in it or might be empty and simply be cruising around to its next designated destination, but there is no requirement that a human driver be present. In fact, the odds are that the Level 5 won't have any driving controls for humans, thus, any human driver is precluded from driving regardless of their interest or willingness to drive.

Level 4 consists of cars that can self-drive in stipulated limited circumstances, formally known as Operational Design Domains (ODD). An ODD might be that the driverless car is okay in dry weather and confined to a geofenced suburb area, which means that once the rain starts falling or you want to visit your relatives in another state, the driverless car won't go. That's not the kind of driverless car that we would likely agree is truly self-driving.

Level 3 and Level 2 are not really self-driving cars at all, since they require that a human licensed driver be present and be able to handle the driving task, co-sharing the wheel with the automation. Some like to refer to these as semi-autonomous cars, though the attempt to qualify the word "autonomous" can be misleading and suggest autonomy that really doesn't fully exist.

Experts in the automotive world tend to rightfully describe Level 2 and Level 3 cars as having ADAS (Advanced Driver-Assistance Systems). A human driver must not only be in the driver's seat, they need to be alert and continually ready to takeover the wheel. The ADAS might suddenly toss the driving back into the human's lap, or the human driver might notice something amiss with the ADAS and yank back control.

With ADAS, at any moment, throughout a driving journey, the human driver must be attentive. For the existing Level 2 and Level 3 cars, those videos you see of drivers sleeping or reading a book, well, those are human drivers that are driving on the edge of calamity and misery. Whether they grasp their predicament or not, they are nonetheless undercutting their part of the co-sharing bargain. It's a recipe for disaster and will be heightened as Level 3 cars emerge and become prevalent.

In a bit of irony, the more advanced the ADAS becomes, the more likely human drivers will become inattentive, lulled into believing that the car is a true self-driving car (but, it's not).

Clarifying When A Rose Is a Rose

Banner headlines often make use of the alluring sounding self-driving, driverless, and robot car monikers, yet this is a blanket style of name-calling that muddies the matter. This might also explain why the general public is a bit confused about the varying claims of self-driving cars. A rose is not a rose by any other name, if it is really an orchid or a sunflower.

It could be that the Level 4 cars that are currently being tried out on our roadways, doing so in limited areas and in limited ways, will validate progress toward true Level 5 self-driving cars. If so, those Level 4 cars are a harbinger of the vaunted Level 5 and therefore you are possibly seeing an early image of what a Level 5 will look like. Or, there might be aspects that require a departure from the Level 4 and researchers must find other ways to bolt together a Level 5.

Astrophysicists have said that putting together the first-ever picture of a black hole, sitting at the center of galaxy Messier 87 (M87), took a tremendous amount of research and effort, even though it might seem as though they merely clicked a button on a camera and snapped a handy photo of the swirling mass of dust and gas.

I assure you that creating a true Level 5 driverless car is still a distance away, maybe not as far away as the M87, but we are not yet there, and the full instant-photo picture of a road-ready Level 5 is still somewhat fuzzy and a bit out-of-focus.

CHAPTER 6

BOEING 737 LESSONS
AND
AI SELF-DRIVING CARS

CHAPTER 6

BOEING 737 LESSONS

AND

AI SELF-DRIVING CAR

The difficulties facing the Boeing 737 MAX 8 have dominated the airline industry news of late and the story about what went wrong and how to fix it are still evolving. At this stage, it is nonetheless possible to leverage what has so far emerged to draw a parallel to the self-driving driverless car realm, allowing for insightful lessons learned about the MAX, the hard way, as an aid and forewarning about autonomous car development.

As indicated by noted philosopher George Santayana, those who cannot learn from history are doomed to repeat it.

Boeing 737 MAX Particulars

The Boeing 737 has been around since the late 1960s and has evolved over time, leading to the NG (Next Generation) series of the 1990s and then the MAX series became the successor to the NG. Boeing opted to retrofit the 737 for the MAX series by mounting the engines further forward and higher than the prior designs.

This tended to potentially cause an upward pitching effect in some flight circumstances, and so a new hardware/software system was added to push the nose down when presumably desired, a system known as MCAS (Maneuvering Characteristics Augmentation System).

The question arises as to when should the MCAS try to push down the nose of the plane, a quite serious action and one that needs to be undertaken with great care and rationale. The computer hardware and software of MCAS would need to know the angle of the plane to ascertain whether a nose down nudge might be warranted, and thus the Angle of Attack (AOA) sensors mounted on the plane were chosen to provide such data to MCAS.

On paper, this all sounds hunky-dory. Seemingly good news, an added system to augment the human pilots and aid in dealing with a known characteristic of the plane. Makes sense.

As with most things in life, though, the devil is in the details. You can implement this overall notion in a multitude of ways, some of which might be more, or less, a capable and suitable feature. Tough design choices come to play. Currently, there are various governmental efforts underway to trace how the particular approach of implementation was determined, which will likely provide added lessons learned.

You are undoubtedly aware that the Boeing 737 MAX 8 was sadly involved in two fatal crashes, one on October 29, 2018, which was Lion Air flight 610, and another fatal crash on March 10, 2019, the Ethiopian Airlines flight 302.

So far, it appears that the MCAS was integral to those two crashes.

Lessons Learned For Driverless Cars

There are actually several lessons already that can be gleaned from what is known today about the situation, or at least what has been reported in the media about the matter.

Even if there are later reports that opt to recast what was previously thought, or add new elements, you can still consider these lessons as worthwhile to observe, regardless of their veracity specific to the Boeing 737 MAX 8.

• Retrofits Versus Starting Anew

Some have pointed fingers at the retrofit of the NG and suggested that the choice of engine placement for the MAX led to a "problem" that never should have arisen (the nose upward pitching effect), which presumably a start-from-scratch approach would have not had.

You might be under the belief that driverless cars are not prone to a retrofit since they are so new, but you'd be mistaken. Many of the driverless car designs of today are based on prior designs, logically so, attempting to build upon what already works.

Lesson #1: Auto makers and tech firms making driverless cars need to be mindful of how their retrofits can be a boon or a bane in terms of the autonomous capability and safety.

• Sensors Criticality

It has been reported that apparently the MCAS relied on just one of the two AOA sensors on the plane, rather than trying to use both, and that the MCAS might have been misled by a faulty AOA sensor reading, telling MCAS a higher angle than true and spurring MCAS to push the nose downward, doing so needlessly and worse so dangerously.

For driverless cars, they are chock full of sensors, cameras aplenty, radar, ultra-sonic sensors, LIDAR (light and radar), and so on. They are the eyes and ears of the autonomous car, without which the self-driving car is blind and would be a frantic menace to all while in-motion.

Lesson #2: Driverless cars need to employ multiple sensors that act redundantly in case any or some of them falter or fail, there should not be any single point-of-failures that can doom the driving effort.

Lesson #3: The sensor fusion that attempts to combine together the sensor readings needs to do so with aplomb, identifying which sensors are working properly and which are misreporting the driving environment, and not become fooled or misled by out-of-whack sensors.

• Human Factors Given Their Due

There is controversy associated with the piloting of the Boeing 737 MAX in that some contend that the pilots might not have had sufficient training about the MCAS aspects, plus the MCAS was apparently setup to proceed without necessarily alerting the pilot (an add-on), and the MCAS was given wide latitude of how often and how far it could nudge down the nose of the plane on its own. These are vital design choices that relate to the Human Factors involved in co-sharing the human-machine flying effort.

For driverless cars less than a Level 5 (Level 5 is the highest level and considered true autonomy that does not require the presence of a human driver), the lesser levels are essentially co-sharing the driving task, similar in a manner to how a pilot might co-share the flying with the MCAS.

Lesson #4: The driverless car when co-sharing needs to ensure that the human driver is aware of what the automation is doing versus what the human is expected to do, it's a somber life-minding dance for both parties.

Lesson #5: It needs to be abundantly clear as to what training the human driver needs for the driving co-sharing effort, and the training has to be undertaken and reinforced over time.

Lesson #6: Design choices for co-shared human-machine driverless cars must take into account human driver frailties, including lack of human attention to the task, human speed-of-response to urgencies, etc.

Conclusion

I've touched upon just some of the key lessons learned based on the recent flight tragedies and assure you that there are many more such lessons hidden within the matter.

Beyond using those lessons for improving airplanes and airplane systems, it is important and useful to extend those automation insights into the realm of self-driving driverless cars. Nothing is too big or too small to fail, and it is prudent to consider how failings can hopefully be prevented or mitigated by design and implementation choices made.

CHAPTER 7

PREVIEW TESLA FSD

AND

AI SELF-DRIVING CARS

CHAPTER 7

PREVIEW TESLA FSD

AND

AI SELF-DRIVING CARS

There's been a lot of suspense permeating the news lately. For example, in anticipation of the now released Mueller Report, the suspenseful build-up encompassed a long wait for the reveal, there was rampant speculation about what it consisted of, there were teasers and snippets, a myriad of claims about its possible impacts, and a breathless show-stopping globally echoing chatter once it hit the streets.

To some degree, you can say that this coming Monday's event at Tesla that has Elon Musk slated to unveil the new Tesla Full Self-Driving (FSD) computer fits those same suspenseful characteristics, at least with respect to the auto industry and the future of transportation. It is on-the-edge of your seat suspense, for sure.

Sanity Check Please

Here's what has been happening, which I provide just in case you've not been mired in the rather over-the-top rhetoric and wide-eyed conjecture already.

Tesla is hosting a cleverly coined "Autonomy Investor Day" on Monday, April 22, 2019, which purportedly will showcase their new Full Self-Driving (FSD) system that serves to replace an earlier core computer in Tesla cars, and those attending will be treated to rides in Tesla's outfitted with the FSD. In addition, there will be speeches and apparently an indicative "road map" that lays out the future elements and timetable for the attainment of true driverless capabilities.

Similar to the suspense surrounding the Mueller Report build-up, Tesla has been relatively tight-lipped about what the FSD fully consists of, and the visionary road map is likewise not yet been displayed. As such, industry insiders have been playing ping pong in terms of speculating about what it all is, and what it all means.

Elon Musk has not been bashful about the matter.

Indeed, deploying his usual megaphone capabilities, he's tweeted that the FSD will ultimately free us from the tyranny of driving a car, and during a recent interview at MIT he proclaimed that it is a tennis analogous competition, with game, set, and match by Tesla, in terms of being allegedly ahead of everyone else, presumably meaning even ahead of Waymo, the Google/Alphabet self-driving car entity that's at the forefront of driverless cars.

That's quite a lot of bravado, though nothing beyond the usual showmanship. Plus, notably, Musk added a qualifying remark, indicating he might be wrong about being vastly ahead of everyone else, though the bravado part got the higher billing in the press.

But let's be very clear about something, the Tesla is not a driverless car, as yet, and the new FSD that replaces the old hardware is not going to instantaneously make their cars into a true Level 5 self-driving car. Do not be confused or bewildered by whatever cacophony of fireworks or blaring trumpets you might see about the Monday fanfare.

Having fast core hardware, it's a necessity, but as they say in the rigors of science, you need both necessities and sufficiency's. The FSD in of itself does not satisfy the sufficiency condition. You need the software too. The software that could or might provide a true driverless experience is not being unveiled at the Monday rodeo, and for all practical purposes does not yet even exist, as far as we all know.

This computer boost with the FSD is apparently being accompanied by some amount of added software that besides aiding driving on highways, provides enhanced parking such as the Summon feature that brings the car to you, and potentially city street driving features. It's a booster for Tesla's Autopilot system. That's all exciting. It's wonderful to have progress being made.

It isn't though the end of the game.

The Tesla is still a car that co-shares the driving task with a human driver. In a bit of dangerous irony, the more advanced the automation becomes for co-shared driving, there is a tendency for the human driver to become increasingly complacent, which raises the risks of such equipped cars to get into car accidents due to confusion and hand-off between the human and the automation. Human factors are key.

Succinctly stated, the game of achieving a true driverless car is still underway.

The goal posts are at a substantive distance ahead. It is not the ninth inning. We are not down to the buzzer on making the last basket.

More Twists In The Plot

Apparently, newer Tesla's will come with the FSD, while older models can potentially get the FSD swapped in.

Scuttlebutt among autonomous cars experts ranges from optimism, with some relabeling FSD as Fantastic Self-Driving or Fabulous Self-Driving, while others that are more pessimistic say it is Facade Self-Driving or Foolhardy Self-Driving. Plenty of memes in this.

Rumors are that Tesla is opting to replace the Nvidia chips with ones of their own, based on a proprietary design by Tesla that can supposedly handle 2,000 frames per second of visual data in lieu of previously only handling 20 frames per second. This implies that the faster computer will be able to cope with more vision processing in a much shorter period of time, a key cornerstone toward being adept enough to potentially do true driverless handling.

For Nvidia, this would seem like a bit of a disappointment since they presumably won't have their chips in the core computer for the go-forward models of Tesla. Tesla might now control their own destiny by having gone proprietary, but that's a dual-edged sword since it also means they are essentially digging deeper into the electronics business. Over time, the FSD will undoubtedly need to be enhanced and improved, which means that it's another task on Tesla's already hectic plate, rather than letting a firm with that kind of devoted competency handle such matters for them.

Also, there is still the matter of the sensors on the Tesla, which comes normally equipped with 8 cameras, 12 ultrasonic sensors, and radar, all-together serving as the primary means of detecting the driving environment. One sensory aspect missing, LIDAR (light and radar), which is used by nearly all others seeking to achieve driverless cars, remains as a type of sensor that Musk believes is not needed, though he's qualified that by saying he could be wrong on that aspect, too.

It is as yet unknown and unproven whether the set of sensors that come with an existing Tesla is sufficient, there might be more needed, and the rapid pace of improvement in sensor technology would suggest that at some point those sensors would be considered potentially outdated in capability; if so, the question arises as to how they would be replaced on already delivered Tesla's and the costs in doing so.

An additional tidbit about Monday is that Tesla will be apparently announcing their aim to establish a fleet of Tesla cars, allowing Tesla owners to possibly participate in ridesharing and earn some extra bucks, doing so via their Tesla (once it presumably becomes autonomous), driving people around while the owner works or sleeps. It is a potential money maker for Tesla owners and for Tesla, doubly so, and it will be interesting to see how this resonates with the likes of Uber and Lyft and others in the ridesharing arena.

Conclusion

Monday is not a giant step for mankind. No one is landing on the moon, as yet. Incremental progress is important and let's mark Monday on our calendars as another inch forward.

CHAPTER 8

LIDAR INDUSTRY

AND

AI SELF-DRIVING CARS

CHAPTER 8

LIDAR INDUSTRY

AND

AI SELF-DRIVING CARS

The popular *Games of Thrones* series has a famed reputation for killing off characters of the provocative cable show, including primary characters, resulting in a rabid fan base that's both on edge and yet eager or entranced to see who lives and who dies. It's the same for those that are watching intently the makers of LIDAR, a type of sensor that combines light and radar, and for which some believe that any true driverless car will require, though, in a mesmerizing plot twist, some say LIDAR is categorically unnecessary for self-driving cars.

If you believe in the necessity of LIDAR to get us to the vaunted Level 5, a true driverless car that works autonomously and no human driver is needed, you are also signing up to believe that LIDAR units will sell like hotcakes.

LIDAR sensors emit a laser beam that bounces off objects surrounding a driverless car and returns those light waves back to the sensor in a radar-like manner, allowing the AI system to construct a 3D model of what might be around the self-driving car, offering crucial clues about what needs to be accounted for during the AI driving task.

Everyone agrees that cameras, a passive kind of sensor, are needed for driverless cars, and many believe that LIDAR, an active kind of sensor leveraging laser beams, provides a significant and perhaps necessary complement to the incontestable visual cameras approach.

Potential Bonanza In LIDAR Sales Volume

The reason to care about LIDAR is due to three enticing words, volume, volume, volume.

Simply stated, having even just one LIDAR unit per every driverless car would suggest that of the 270 million cars in the US today, assuming they all such conventional autos would get replaced by self-driving cars, implies that correspondingly there would be 270 million LIDAR units required. That's a whopping lot of units of anything, and a boon larger than the zombie-like White Walkers and marching forward in *Game of Thrones*.

Worldwide today, there are over 1 billion cars, and imagine if they were all ultimately replaced by true driverless cars, it would amount to selling over 1 billion LIDAR units. Plus, don't forget about replacement units needed for when those LIDAR units gradually wear out or falter from time-to-time. Furthermore, rather than just one LIDAR unit per driverless car, it might end-up that there could be several adornments per vehicle, creating a handy multiplier effect on the number of units needed.

Those are the kinds of numbers that get VC/PE firms salivating, aiming for a type of tech that can knock it out of the ballpark.

Keep in mind too that LIDAR isn't confined to just aiding driverless cars. You can use LIDAR for lots of other applications, essentially any kind of robot that might need to detect its surroundings, along with using LIDAR in factories and warehouses. The driverless car is the shiny object of attention for LIDAR, but there's a much greater game at play. That's how things go in any notable game of thrones.

LIDAR Makers Aplenty

This realization of the market potential for LIDAR has stoked a gold rush by electronics makers that want into this epic battle.

One of the pioneers of LIDAR, Velodyne, which got into the game early, continues to be the comparison metric for others that are now emerging in this niche (I attended their driverless car industry safety summit last year, one of the first to host such an event, getting a chance to see up close their vision for the future). For those of you that might have seen me at CES in January 2019, I admittedly looked disheveled and worn out, having tried to visit each of the LIDAR vendors presenting their wares at the Vegas extravaganza, including vendors such as Robosense, Innoviz, SOS Lab, Quanergy, AEye, LG Electronics, Bajara, OPSYS, Leddartech, Cepton, Ouster, Luminar, V elodyne, and many others.

In *Game of Thrones* there is a continual struggle of kings and queens all vying to rule particular lands and possibly be the grandest ruler of all, which is an apt analogy to the LIDAR scene today.

There are daily pronouncements by the now hordes of LIDAR vendors as to their particular LIDAR being the best in some capability or feature, such as fastest at time-of-flight, or least number of moving parts, or most reliable, or least costly, etc. Last month, Google/Alphabet's Waymo self-driving car entity, announced they are selling their homebrewed LIDAR sensors, though restricted to non-car uses to keep from handing the keys to the kingdom to their direct competition.

The fierce and unrelenting competition in LIDAR has fostered a heathy spate of new breakthroughs and advances. LIDAR units used to be in the six-figure cost range, and now dip below $100,000, including units below $10,000 and even underneath $1,000. Be cautious though in comparing LIDAR sensors, since by cost alone you don't know what the sensor can really do, you might be getting a scaled-down feature-lite version for your money that will only work in quite limited ways.

Cliff Hanger - Is LIDAR Needed For Driverless Cars

Here's the mind-bending plot twist about LIDAR, perhaps as shocking as last year's *Game of Thrones* monumental death of (spoiler alert!) Littlefinger, namely that there is a small contingent that believes LIDAR is not a necessity for achieving true driverless cars.

The most notable and vocal contrarian would be Elon Musk, fervently stating on Tesla earnings calls that LIDAR is unnecessary and insistent that the latest Tesla cars already have all the sensors they need for Level 5.

I tend to believe that LIDAR is a necessity and that Level 5 won't happen without it. Musk has stated that he might be mistaken about the lack of a need for LIDAR, opening the door to the possibility of its utility, which showcases that the contrarian crowd is somewhat hesitant on the matter. Even if LIDAR isn't a pure necessity, and driverless car makers somehow over-engineer and use LIDAR when it in fact is not needed per se, one view is that it is a capable third-hand (like the three-eyed raven in *Thrones*), providing a safety boost that non-LIDAR using Level 5 cars would lack.

Now that season 8 of *Games of Thrones* is underway, the seemingly endless supply of plot predictions about what will happen are going to play out over the six prized episodes of this final season. Likewise, predictions about whether LIDAR is needed or not for Level 5 will play out as the auto makers and tech firms reach for the stars and seek to craft a true driverless car. One thing for sure, it is not going to be a live-happily-ever-after for the throngs of LIDAR makers, and it is a sure bet some of them won't survive.

That's a spoiler alert.

CHAPTER 9

UBER IPO

AND

AI SELF-DRIVING CARS

CHAPTER 9

UBER IPO

AND

AI SELF-DRIVING CARS

It is that time of the year for high schoolers to be getting primped and primed for their prom night, trying to ensure that their hair is groomed just right, and they've got in-hand the finest sociably fashionable clothes and are otherwise ready-to-go for the biggest night of the lives.

You could say that Uber is doing the same for their upcoming prom-like IPO, hoping to look glitzy and ready-to-go.

While pitching investors, Uber needs to be as primped and primed as it can be. They want to be magnificently alluring for their biggest night, well, day, when they launch into the public stocks stratosphere. Their effort though to get dolled-up is potentially daunting due to a number of seemingly less bejeweled aspects that the media has been fretting over.

Notably, the firm continues to burn through an enormous amount of cash and still is posting gargantuan operating losses. In their formal filings, the company acknowledged that their ridesharing marketplace position declined last year in a substantial majority of their targeted markets. There's the ruthless and unrelenting competition to factor into their status.

There's the anti-fanbase pushing for us all to #DeleteUber, there's the roller coaster of Lyft's IPO results that some say could be a sign that Uber could get hammered and oddly enough because Lyft potently revealed that ridesharing isn't all wine and roses (one nagging question, could their mainstay competitor have dampened investor enthusiasm, by being the first out-the-gate, and laying bare the untoward underbelly that undercuts the perceived ridesharing nirvana).

Perhaps one of the savviest preening acts by Uber so far is the recently announced $1 billion investment by SoftBank Group Corporation, along with Toyota Motor Corporation and Denso Corporation, pumping cash into Uber Technologies Incorporated for the honor of being immersed into Uber's self-driving driverless car efforts.

A strategically smart move, containing a hidden message that many have not yet detected.

The Coopetition Deal

The most obvious rationale for Uber to make the investment deal involves the valuation aspects.

The billion-dollar table-stakes implies that the Uber self-driving car unit is worth around $7.25B, according to industry analyses, and helps to support a potential IPO that's aiming to raise around $10 billion and value Uber overall at about $100 billion. Logically, if these big-time and highly successful companies are willing to put a sizable chunk-of-change into Uber, it provides a nice afterglow of the presumed strength and value of the firm.

Furthermore, for those that might be worried that the ongoing cash drain from the Uber self-driving car efforts might be a false hope, you've now got the confidence builder by the three cheerleaders willing to put their money on-the-line. Apparently, Uber will reportedly be spinning out the self-driving car unit, encompassing six board seats for Uber and one each for SoftBank and Toyota.

This kind of coopetition has been rampant in the self-driving car realm. Firms that might be considered competitors, depending upon your vantage point, have been coming together in a myriad of cooperative arrangements.

Why would they do so? Because self-driving driverless cars are no piece-of-cake to make and field.

It's hard, it's costly, and it is going to take longer than some pundits and prognosticators claim. If you didn't need to strike a coopetition deal, you normally wouldn't do so, wanting to hang onto the pie all yourself. Typically, coopetition's happen when firms realize that they are biting off more than they can chew, or essentially are willing to spread around the risk.

You could say that the billion-dollar investment is actually a kind of insurance policy. Allow me to elaborate.

Reading Between The Lines

Besides the seemingly noticeable aspect of boosting the esteem of Uber and bolstering its self-driving car pursuits, along with getting an influx of added expertise and viewpoint, plus the cash to keep the driverless car R&D engine going, there's the dispersion of risk.

Recall, sadly, there was the Uber self-driving car incident in Tempe, Arizona last year that involved the death of a pedestrian, being struck by an Uber self-driving car that had a back-up driver present and the event raised both national and even global concerns about the status and readiness of autonomous cars.

Uber temporarily suspended its roadway trials and conducted a safety check, ultimately issuing a report of what Uber will be doing henceforth for their self-driving efforts. They quietly and somewhat reservedly resumed their roadway trials, doing so in Pittsburgh.

There's a well-known rule-of-thumb in the systems field that you can have one bad instance when doing an initial rollout or trial of some kind, and many will consider it a fluke, giving you some breathing room to try again, but if you have a second such adverse instance, the hammer will come down, mercilessly.

In some respects, the Boeing 737 MAX highlights that rule-of-thumb, notably that the first crash involving the MCAS system issue had a relatively modest reaction overall, while the second crash led to a cataclysmic reaction.

Right now, as Uber is undertaking their daily tryouts of their self-driving cars, even in the limited scope underway, they are on the precipice of a dicey and cataclysmic second potential incident. No matter how low the chances of such a second instance, the impact if it occurred would be enormous.

In short, if there is perchance a second deadly incident, and it occurs between now and their IPO, the reaction could be so massive that it could undermine the nature of the IPO, including its size and timing. Some might protest and say that the self-driving car unit would be like the tail wagging the dog, namely that the firm shouldn't be overall penalized by such an unfortunate added adverse instance in their fledgling autonomous car effort, but you can pretty much bet that the vitriolic reaction would not discern that kind of nuance.

How can a firm in such a posture of already having incurred one such woeful instance be able deal with the matter?

You might suggest that they summarily halt their driverless car tryouts, thereby preventing entirely a second instance from happening, and wait to continue until after the IPO.

No, that won't fly.

It would be tantamount to suggesting they are unsure about their self-driving possibilities, usurping a key element of the firm and something that most believe ties integrally to the future of the firm. It would certainly puncture a hole in the valuation balloon to simply stop the tryouts right now and would raise rather vexatious questions.

Instead, the coopetition path provides a means to cope with the matter.

If a second instance were to occur, let's all hope not, there is now a possibility of indicating that the added partners were brought on-board to aid in preventing such instances and can bring to the table a capability and sensibility to overcome whatever issue or flaw allowed the second instance. Moreover, by spinning out the entity, it gives the parent firm a bit more room to be distanced from the wrath that would undoubtedly roil the driverless car unit.

It's a dispersion of risk, an insurance policy that had been subtlety and discretely put in place, prudently established, just-in-case, and happened to fortunately have other beneficial qualities too.

Conclusion

Companies need to be considering their contingencies and be ready for whatever roll of the dice happens. The billion-dollar investment into Uber for a stake in their autonomous car effort has lots of benefits to Uber, especially right now, while getting ready for their IPO prom.

The hidden element that I've articulated provides an added bonus to offset risk, though presumably and hopefully no such incident will arise, and like any insurance policy, you are usually hoping that your never need to file an insurance claim and invoke your surety.

CHAPTER 10

SUING AUTOMAKERS

AND

AI SELF-DRIVING CARS

CHAPTER 10

SUING AUTOMAKERS
AND
AI SELF-DRIVING CARS

The driving task is both a blessing and a curse. We'll ultimately determine more so which prevails, inexorably, when lawsuits and court cases emerge involving autonomous and semi-autonomous cars. As cars become increasingly automated, I'm predicting that the number of lawsuits and legal wrangling will undoubtedly blossom too. There's no free lunch in the delivery of self-driving cars.

During Tesla's Autonomy Investor Day, a question was asked of Elon Musk about his proposed ridesharing fleet approach of Tesla autonomous cars, which would include Tesla's owned by individuals, and the question was about who would be liable if a Tesla autonomous car in the fleet get into a car accident. Musk seemed somewhat taken aback by the question, considered it for a moment, and then said it would be Tesla, though his answer was somewhat hesitatingly stated.

His pause was quite understandable, since we are entering into rather uncharted waters on such matters.

Let's consider why.

First, consider the nature of driving a car. Dynamic Driving Task (DDT) is the formal parlance in the autonomous car realm and refers to the act of driving a car, including all of the tactical and operational mechanizations such as steering, acceleration, deceleration, object detection and avoidance, maneuvering, and the like. Humans are the mainstay of DDT today. A human watches the road ahead, steers the car, punches the brakes, hits the accelerator, and otherwise exercises a kind of superpower to drive a car.

Though this superpower is not the same as those of notable fictional characters such as Superman, Superwoman, Shazam, and Wonder Woman, it nonetheless is a remarkable feat that humans seem to be able to undertake, properly, most of the time. The act of driving, which you likely believe is a somewhat trivial task (some say it's not brain surgery), actually involves a miraculous set of capabilities that are quite hard to fully automate.

Semi-Autonomous Means Co-Sharing The Driving Task

Cars that are semi-autonomous involve a co-sharing effort of having the human and the automated system drive the car, together, usually referred to as providing ADAS (Advanced Driver Assistance Systems), alleviating some aspects of the DDT from the shoulders of the human driver. These semi-automated cars are considered less than a true self-driving car, which is labeled as a Level 5, the topmost level that does not require the presence of a human driver in the car.

Here's the lawsuit danger zone for the ADAS co-shared driving cars.

When there is a car accident involving a semi-autonomous car, who is at fault? The immediate and so far proffered answer is that it is the human driver. In the co-sharing arrangement, the assumption is that the human driver is ultimately responsible for the driving of the car. One might liken this to the notion that it is the captain of the ship that holds ultimate responsibility for the vessel, regardless of what else might have transpired that led to a crash or sinking.

It is not so apparent that this kind of "standard" will inevitably hold for semi-autonomous cars. Right now, we are seeing the emergence of Level 3 semi-autonomous cars, having an increasing capability to do lane changes, drive on city streets, and the like. In spite of those advances, the human driver is still considered in-charge, at least that's what the auto makers and tech firms say, but do the human driver's grasp this?

Ironically, as the automation gets better, it lulls or entices the human driver into assuming that they have no need to drive the car, actively, and can be an inattentive partner in the driving task. You've seen those videos of human drivers that are watching TV or tapping on their smartphones, seemingly ignoring the realities of the road and the driving effort. This is setting up a quite dangerous situation. The automation might need sudden help, involving a split-second driving decision and immediate action by the human driver, and yet the human is engrossed in the latest episode of their favorite cable show.

It is a recipe for disaster.

Product Liability Enters Into The Picture

In the United States, there are three core ways to seek a product liability claim, consisting of:

- Failure to adequately forewarn about proper use
- Defective design of the product
- Defective manufacturing of the product

For the Level 3 semi-autonomous cars, the question is going to be asked as to whether or not the auto maker or tech firm provided adequate forewarning about how to properly use the car, meaning that the human driver was sufficiently informed about the co-sharing task and their role in driving the car.

Some auto makers are adding devices to detect whether the human driver is paying attention to the driving task, such as a camera pointing at the eyes of the driver or a steering wheel that senses their hand pressure, but will this be enough? Will indicating too that the owner's manual spells out your duties as a human driver be considered adequate forewarning (some say it is customary to ignore your owner's manual or toss it aside)?

If your conventional car gets rammed by a human driver in a Level 3 car and the driver was evidently not attending to the driving, besides going after that inattentive driver, you presumably might go after the auto maker or tech firm for having missed the mark on ensuring that their product adequately alerted about how it was to be properly used by the human driver.

In lieu of the forewarning provision, or in addition to it, you might claim that the auto maker or tech firm had a defective design in their product. Suppose the automation was supposed to alert the human driver that a crash was going to occur, allowing them to take corrective action, and the designers opted to code the automation in a manner that it took say four seconds to provide such an alert. This four second provision might be shown as being a flawed design choice, and perhaps studies showed that it should have been two seconds instead, but that's not the choice the designers made.

There could also be defective manufacturing involved, such as the sensors on the car that detect an object ahead were perhaps improperly installed when the Level 3 car was made.

Level 5 Driverless Car Proneness To Liability

Some of the auto makers or tech firms are aiming to jump past the lower levels and aim for a Level 5 car, partially and purposefully to try and avoid the dicey co-sharing driving quagmire. At the Level 5, there is no question that the car is supposed to be driven by the automation and there is ergo no driving per se by a human driver. That settles the question about whether the human driver is at fault in a Level 5, no, since there isn't a provision for human driving therein.

If there is an AI system or automation that is doing the Level 5 driving, does that mean that the automation is sentient and somehow responsible, all by itself, as though it is the equivalent of a human driver?

It would be a real stretch of the imagination to make such a claim. The AI systems for driving a car are not a life-form "being" and we are likely quite far away from seeing AI that can be considered sentient (hint, I'm not a "singularity any day now" kind of advocate, nor do I buy into the AI doomsday notions, for now).

Though there is ongoing debate about who will be responsible for a Level 5's driving actions, the cast of likely suspects can already be ascertained.

It could be the auto maker of the Level 5 car and the tech developers, since they were the designers and builders of the Level 5 AI system of the driverless car. It could be the owner of the Level 5 car, whether it is a fleet owner or individually owned. It could be a combination of them, sharing the burden. It assuredly is not going to be the AI itself, even if the AI has some kind of Machine Learning or Deep Learning included.

Conclusion

The focus on who's responsible comes down to the AI as a form of automation and whether it was defectively manufactured, or defectively designed, or failed to forewarn about proper use. Maybe in some faraway future we'll have devised AI that can think on its own in a sentient manner, and you can try suing it, but rest assured that's not what the AI of today's emerging Level 5 cars are doing and they aren't going to be sitting in the witness chair on their own, anytime soon.

CHAPTER 11

TESLA OVERARCHING FSD

AND

AI SELF-DRIVING CARS

CHAPTER 11

TESLA OVERARCHING FSD

AND

AI SELF-DRIVING CARS

"Sometimes, I'm not on time," conceded Elon Musk at today's Autonomy Investor Day, an event that was undertaken by Tesla to showcase their progress on their Full Self-Driving (FSD) efforts (side-note: I had promised readers in my Friday posting that I'd follow-up today with a review and provide key takeaways, so here it is).

He wasn't referring to the late start of the event (it got underway about 30-minutes later than scheduled), but instead he was responding to questions about his bold and brash claim that Tesla will be considered so-called "feature complete," apparently meaning being at a true Level 5 driverless status, later this year, and that human drivers will be able to go completely hands-free and eyes-closed by the second quarter of next year.

The palatable sense of disbelief about such timing, notably that the vaunted Level 5 could be achieved in such a short time by Tesla, prompted Musk's concessionary comment, though he emphasized that in spite of at times being wrong on his schedule-targeted predictions, he asserted that he ultimately does get the job done.

Some might liken Musk's enthusiasm to his earlier efforts to make a hyper-automated factory of the future for producing his cars, and later on, after great difficulties in automating human-based car-assembly tasks, he acknowledged that humans are underrated.

Driving a car, which seems trivial to most, can often times be underrated as a type of task that humans are generally able to perform.

Overall, there was nothing today that showcased proof that Tesla cars will be performing as true Level 5 driverless car this year, nor next year, nor any time soon.

No Indicated Path To Level 5 In Near-Term

The event offered fascinating details about the new homemade neural network hardware chips being used in Tesla's outfitted with the latest FSD, dropping out the use of Nvidia chips, but unfortunately the portions of the presentation on the software side of things were quite wanting in terms of providing any definitive evidence that Level 5 is around the corner.

You are not going to hardware-alone your way to becoming a Level 5. It's a completeness and sufficiency matter, requiring both the right hardware and the right software.

For those attending that were not versed in the tech of self-driving cars, it was perhaps instructive to get the sophomore-level tutorial about the fundamentals of neural networks and Machine Learning, but for those of us versed in such matters, it was like sitting through a Self-Driving Car 101 class, offering little of any meaty substance to sift through.

I am particularly worried that those unfamiliar with such technology will fall victim to believing that they saw the advent of Level 5.

Let's be clear, there was essentially no attention paid to the numerous and known flaws and limitations of today's neural networks and Deep Learning. There was also almost no indication of how the FSD incorporates heuristic style programming with neural networks to arrive at a Level 5. In short, the evidence presented was scant on any real details that mattered, in spite of the event lasting nearly three hours.

Having a goal of achieving Level 5 is wonderful, and Musk can be appreciated for his determination to get there but doing so within a year from now requires some kind of bona fide step-by-step depiction to prove or amply showcase how it will be done, otherwise it is cast as more dream than reality.

Slams LIDAR And HD Maps

There were other bold and brash proclamations during the event.

Musk opted to up the ante on his prior assertion that LIDAR, a type of sensor that combines light via lasers and radar, might not be optimal for use with self-driving cars, and flat out said that the use of LIDAR is a false hope and foolish to undertake. He has now tossed down the gauntlet, fully, unabashedly removing any prior hesitation in which he had suggested that someday he might be proven wrong.

This now pits Musk's belief against nearly all other self-driving car makers since just about everyone else is using LIDAR.

He and his team used the now time-worn claim that since humans don't have lasers in their heads, and only eyeballs, presumably the driving task can be done entirely via vision. Meanwhile, it was then mentioned that they are using radar to bolster their vision processing elements. To overcome what certainly seemed like a logical inconsistency in the vision-only argument, they floated a quick series of off-handed remarks about why radar is better than LIDAR.

I don't think that the LIDAR industry needs to close-up shop.

We'll need to wait and see what Tesla's contrarian viewpoint brings forth on LIDAR, though it will certainly be eye opening if Tesla's self-driving cars get into car accidents and how Tesla will defend against a claim that if there had been LIDAR that the accident might not have occurred. Plus, today's comments might have opened a can of worms by offering that LIDAR is too expensive, in addition to stating that LIDAR is unnecessary.

There was also a heavy dose of bashing on the use of High Definition (HD) maps. It was stated that Tesla had started toward using HD maps, and then dropped it, apparently under the belief that HD maps would lead to a driverless system that was too brittle. This is another time-worn argument, suggesting that if you use HD maps that you won't do the other hard work on the rest of the driverless capabilities, which so far does not seem to be the case in the industry.

Some other points were equally debatable, such as the contention that only forward-facing radar is needed (which is how the Tesla's are outfitted, while most other driverless cars have radar units at the sides and backs, or 360-degree radar units). The stated rationale for using just forward-facing radar was that the car is moving fast in that direction.

Yes, we get that, but what about when another car that's coming up from behind you and will ram into your car, it would certainly be handy to have the driverless car watch out for those deadly moments (beyond relying on vision alone).

Other Notable Points

There was an indication about the use of Tesla driverless cars in a fleet manner, which were referred to as robotaxis, allowing Tesla owners to provide their vehicles as part of a ridesharing network, similar to renting out your home via AirBnB, in conjunction with Tesla-owned vehicles also roaming around. This was touted as a huge money maker for both Tesla and Tesla car owners, which indeed makes sense, but the devil is in the details.

In fact, during the Q&A portion, it became apparent that this futuristic approach has not yet been fully figured out, including what would happen when a ridesharing passenger got into such a Tesla car and opted to play with the steering wheel (presumably taking over control of the car).

Imagine that you've summoned a driverless Tesla to the elementary school to pick-up your child and whisk them home, and your rambunctious 8-year-old decides to handle the wheel. Not so good.

According to the presentation, the new FSD has already started rolling out, doing so in March, and for new Tesla Model 3's it began being installed about ten days ago. Musk also announced that Tesla is working on the next generation of their FSD, indicating they are about 2 years away from having it appear, which the only reveal that he offered was that it will be 3x better. I'll keep my eyes peeled for more details as they arise.

Conclusion

You have to say that Elon Musk has a passion and determination that by sheer willpower alone is aiding and spurring the push toward Level 5 self-driving cars. One must also though be mindful of the dangers of moving ahead without having thought through key nuances and considerations, especially with the life-or-death consequences of driverless cars.

CHAPTER 12

AUTO REPAIR MARKET

AND

AI SELF-DRIVING CARS

CHAPTER 12

AUTO REPAIR MARKET
AND
AI SELF-DRIVING CARS

That cha-ching sound of money being made from driverless cars will be the inexorable clatter coming from cash registers ringing over and over at auto repair shops as a bonanza boost is spurred via autonomous car prevalence. I realize that many would be shocked to think that that the advent of driverless cars could actually help auto repair volume, since the prevailing wisdom is that it will have the opposite effect, knocking down the need for car repairs and presumably putting auto repair into the junk heap.

That's some faulty thinking there.

Let's consider why it might seem to the unacquainted that car repairs will be lessening, and then reveal the real truth about why auto repair is going to in-point-of-fact skyrocket.

Pampered Self-Driving Cars Are Among Us

Right now, those vaunted self-driving autonomous Level 5 cars undergoing roadway trials are being overseen by dedicated teams of experts and specialists, doting to every need and whim of the driverless car.

Typically, the revered driverless car is tended with gobs of loving care. Each night, after a tiring day of roaming around for the better part of the day, it gets tucked into a warm and cozy facility that is stocked with every imaginable car repair capability. NASCAR race cars would be envious if they saw what their self-driving car brethren were getting (those race cars might even seek to negotiate a better deal for themselves).

From an outsider perspective, the driverless cars appear to be perpetual motion machines. You would naturally assume that these cars with the newest of everything would work flawlessly, all of the time, and therefore it is a doomsday sign for the auto repair entities.

I'd like to bring us back to the real-world, thanks.

Driverless Cars Once They Are Actually In Use

First, keep in mind that most would agree that self-driving cars are going to be used nearly non-stop, 24 hours per day, 7 days per week, which makes sense for several reasons. Normal car usage is maybe 5% or at most 10% of their availability, since cars usually sit in a parking lot while you are at work or solemnly are inactive in your garage while your head is nestled on your pillow at night.

A traditional car is a woefully under-utilized asset.

The main reason that your car isn't used more is likely due to the lack of an available driver. In the case of driverless cars, the automated driver is always ready and willing to go. No sense in letting an expensive asset be idle and poorly leveraged, thus you'll undoubtedly put the self-driving car into a ridesharing network that can keep it going, and going, and making money, whenever you don't need it for your own needs.

This means that a self-driving car is bound to get many more miles under its belt than a traditional car. A lot more miles. Each day. All day long. And what happens when a car gets a ton of miles? Things go wrong and the car needs repairs.

Wear and tear is a law of physics, no matter how good the AI might be on an autonomous car, it's all still a car.

More miles translate into more wear and tear. Parts are going to need to be replaced.

Ongoing maintenance is going to be keenly desired, especially since the lost revenue from any downtime is going to be hurtful. If your traditional car of today goes sour, you might walk, ride the bus, or find some other means to travel. When your money-making driverless car goes sour, you are going to be quite upset and for each minute and each hour that your valued asset is kaput, you earn nothing.

But There's Even More To Go Wrong (Or Right)

If that isn't already convincing enough for you, I'll add more fuel to the auto repair volcanic fire.

Besides needing to deal with the conventional car elements, there is also the need to deal with the myriad of additional sensors, such as the multiple cameras, the radar units, the ultrasonic units, perhaps the LIDAR units, and the rest. Those are going to breakdown. Each driverless car might have upwards of several dozen high-tech sensors, which suggests the chances of sensor failures and sensor replacements are going to be high, multiplied by however many millions of such cars eventually get onto the roadways.

Since these driverless cars are going to be used for ridesharing, you can bet too that the interiors of the self-driving car will take quite a beating. Think of all those people, getting into and out of the driverless car, hour after hour, all day long, all week long. I doubt these passengers will be mindful of their milkshakes that spill, or their drunken excretion spillovers, and the wear and tear to the insides of the driverless car will be mighty. Once again, it needs to get fixed, otherwise a bad Yelp-like review of your ridesharing autonomous car might get it knocked off the network.

Still not convinced?

There is a plethora of computer processors inside a driverless car, along with banks of computer memory. It is not going to magically work all the time and without hiccup.

Of course, any failure or fault of the AI system core is bad news for the use of the driverless car; plus, since if it won't likely have any driving controls for humans (which is what is being anticipated), the autonomous car becomes a multi-ton paperweight. You can't drive it, even if you were willing as a human to be a stand-in for the AI.

There are scads of electronic communication devices in a driverless car, some for V2V (vehicle-to-vehicle), V2I (vehicle-to-infrastructure), V2P (vehicle-to-pedestrian), OTA (Over-The-Air updating), GPS, and so on. Yes, those will have faults or breakdown too.

It is assumed that most driverless cars will be EVs, which make sense to power all of the electronic gadgetry, but this also tends to imply that there are newer kinds of car components, many of which have not yet stood the test of time. The odds of recalls are likely substantial. Discovering too that some parts breakdown sooner than thought, well, it's quite possible, since those are parts that weren't time tested by traditional cars.

Conclusion

Once there is a preponderance of driverless cars, the auto repair business will be booming, but it will admittedly take a while to get there.

When self-driving cars first gain traction, it will likely be under the guise of major entities that own fleets, but the little guy will want into the action too, and we'll see a cottage industry of everyday individuals starting their own driverless car businesses, a kind of mini-me fleet owner.

The auto dealers will likely get the repair volume in early days, but the split is going to shift over time and the independent auto shops will get their due.

Another way to think of that shiny new driverless car that sits in the dealership showrooms (once that happens), it offers great promise, especially after it gets roadway use and promises to have wear and tear, recalls, breakdowns, and be an insatiable maintenance temptress.

Promising for auto repair shops, though maybe not as thrilling to the owners of those extoled autonomous cars.

APPENDIX

APPENDIX A

TEACHING WITH THIS MATERIAL

The material in this book can be readily used either as a supplemental to other content for a class, or it can also be used as a core set of textbook material for a specialized class. Classes where this material is most likely used include any classes at the college or university level that want to augment the class by offering thought provoking and educational essays about AI and self-driving cars.

In particular, here are some aspects for class use:

o   Computer Science. Studying AI, autonomous vehicles, etc.

o   Business. Exploring technology and it adoption for business.

o   Sociology. Sociological views on the adoption and advancement of technology.

Specialized classes at the undergraduate and graduate level can also make use of this material.

For each chapter, consider whether you think the chapter provides material relevant to your course topic. There is plenty of opportunity to get the students thinking about the topic and force them to decide whether they agree or disagree with the points offered and positions taken. I would also encourage you to have the students do additional research beyond the chapter material presented (I provide next some suggested assignments they can do).

RESEARCH ASSIGNMENTS ON THESE TOPICS

Your students can find background material on these topics, doing so in various business and technical publications. I list below the top ranked AI related journals. For business publications, I would suggest the usual culprits such as the Harvard Business Review, Forbes, Fortune, WSJ, and the like.

Here are some suggestions of homework or projects that you could assign to students:

a) <u>Assignment for foundational AI research topic</u>: Research and prepare a paper and a presentation on a specific aspect of Deep AI, Machine Learning, ANN, etc. The paper should cite at least 3 reputable sources. Compare and contrast to what has been stated in this book.

b) <u>Assignment for the Self-Driving Car topic</u>: Research and prepare a paper and Self-Driving Cars. Cite at least 3 reputable sources and analyze the characterizations. Compare and contrast to what has been stated in this book.

c) <u>Assignment for a Business topic</u>: Research and prepare a paper and a presentation on businesses and advanced technology. What is hot, and what is not? Cite at least 3 reputable sources. Compare and contrast to the depictions in this book.

d) <u>Assignment to do a Startup:</u> Have the students prepare a paper about how they might startup a business in this realm. They must submit a sound Business Plan for the startup. They could also be asked to present their Business Plan and so should also have a presentation deck to coincide with it.

You can certainly adjust the aforementioned assignments to fit to your particular needs and the class structure. You'll notice that I ask for 3 reputable cited sources for the paper writing based assignments. I usually steer students toward "reputable" publications, since otherwise they will cite some oddball source that has no credentials other than that they happened to write something and post it onto the Internet. You can define "reputable" in whatever way you prefer, for example some faculty think Wikipedia is not reputable while others believe it is reputable and allow students to cite it.

The reason that I usually ask for at least 3 citations is that if the student only does one or two citations they usually settle on whatever they happened to find the fastest. By requiring three citations, it usually seems to force them to look around, explore, and end-up probably finding five or more, and then whittling it down to 3 that they will actually use.

I have not specified the length of their papers, and leave that to you to tell the students what you prefer. For each of those assignments, you could end-up with a short one to two pager, or you could do a dissertation length paper. Base the length on whatever best fits for your class, and the credit amount of the assignment within the context of the other grading metrics you'll be using for the class.

I mention in the assignments that they are to do a paper and prepare a presentation. I usually try to get students to present their work. This is a good practice for what they will do in the business world. Most of the time, they will be required to prepare an analysis and present it. If you don't have the class time or inclination to have the students present, then you can of course cut out the aspect of them putting together a presentation.

If you want to point students toward highly ranked journals in AI, here's a list of the top journals as reported by *various citation counts sources* (this list changes year to year):

- Communications of the ACM
- Artificial Intelligence
- Cognitive Science
- IEEE Transactions on Pattern Analysis and Machine Intelligence
- Foundations and Trends in Machine Learning
- Journal of Memory and Language
- Cognitive Psychology
- Neural Networks
- IEEE Transactions on Neural Networks and Learning Systems
- IEEE Intelligent Systems
- Knowledge-based Systems

GUIDE TO USING THE CHAPTERS

For each of the chapters, I provide next some various ways to use the chapter material. You can assign the tasks as individual homework assignments, or the tasks can be used with team projects for the class. You can easily layout a series of assignments, such as indicating that the students are to do item "a" below for say Chapter 1, then "b" for the next chapter of the book, and so on.

a) What is the main point of the chapter and describe in your own words the significance of the topic,

b) Identify at least two aspects in the chapter that you agree with, and support your concurrence by providing at least one other outside researched item as support; make sure to explain your basis for disagreeing with the aspects,

c) Identify at least two aspects in the chapter that you disagree with, and support your disagreement by providing at least one other outside researched item as support; make sure to explain your basis for disagreeing with the aspects,

d) Find an aspect that was not covered in the chapter, doing so by conducting outside research, and then explain how that aspect ties into the chapter and what significance it brings to the topic,

e) Interview a specialist in industry about the topic of the chapter, collect from them their thoughts and opinions, and readdress the chapter by citing your source and how they compared and contrasted to the material,

f) Interview a relevant academic professor or researcher in a college or university about the topic of the chapter, collect from them their thoughts and opinions, and readdress the chapter by citing your source and how they compared and contrasted to the material,

g) Try to update a chapter by finding out the latest on the topic, and ascertain whether the issue or topic has now been solved or whether it is still being addressed, explain what you come up with.

The above are all ways in which you can get the students of your class involved in considering the material of a given chapter. You could mix things up by having one of those above assignments per each week, covering the chapters over the course of the semester or quarter.

As a reminder, here are the chapters of the book and you can select whichever chapters you find most valued for your particular class:

Chapter Title

1   Eliot Framework for AI Self-Driving Cars   15

2   Zero Knowledge Proofs and AI Self-Driving Cars   29

3   Active Shooter Response and AI Self-Driving Cars   61

4   Free Will and AI Self-Driving Cars   83

5   No Picture Yet of AI Self-Driving Cars   107

6   Boeing 737 Lessons and AI Self-Driving Cars   113

7   Preview Tesla FSD and AI Self-Driving Cars   121

8   LIDAR Industry and AI Self-Driving Cars   129

9   Uber IPO and AI Self-Driving Cars   135

10   Suing Automakers of AI Self-Driving Cars   143

11   Tesla Overarching FSD and AI Self-Driving Cars   151

12   Auto Repair Market and AI Self-Driving Cars   159

Companion Book By This Author

Advances in AI and Autonomous Vehicles: Cybernetic Self-Driving Cars

Practical Advances in Artificial Intelligence (AI) and Machine Learning

by

Dr. Lance B. Eliot, MBA, PhD

Chapter Title

1 Genetic Algorithms for Self-Driving Cars
2 Blockchain for Self-Driving Cars
3 Machine Learning and Data for Self-Driving Cars
4 Edge Problems at Core of True Self-Driving Cars
5 Solving the Roundabout Traversal Problem for SD Cars
6 Parallel Parking Mindless Task for SD Cars: Step It Up
7 Caveats of Open Source for Self-Driving Cars
8 Catastrophic Cyber Hacking of Self-Driving Cars
9 Conspicuity for Self-Driving Cars
10 Accident Scene Traversal for Self-Driving Cars
11 Emergency Vehicle Awareness for Self-Driving Cars
12 Are Left Turns Right for Self-Driving Cars
13 Going Blind: When Sensors Fail on Self-Driving Cars
14 Roadway Debris Cognition for Self-Driving Cars
15 Avoiding Pedestrian Roadkill by Self-Driving Cars
16 When Accidents Happen to Self-Driving Cars
17 Illegal Driving for Self-Driving Cars
18 Making AI Sense of Road Signs
19 Parking Your Car the AI Way
20 Not Fast Enough: Human Factors in Self-Driving Cars
21 State of Government Reporting on Self-Driving Cars
22 The Head Nod Problem for Self-Driving Cars
23 CES Reveals Self-Driving Car Differences

This title is available via Amazon and other book sellers

Companion Book By This Author

Self-Driving Cars:
"The Mother of All AI Projects"

by Dr. Lance B. Eliot, MBA, PhD

Chapter Title

1 Grand Convergence Explains Rise of Self-Driving Cars

2 Here is Why We Need to Call Them Self-Driving Cars

3 Richter Scale for Levels of Self-Driving Cars

4 LIDAR as Secret Sauce for Self-Driving Cars

5 Pied Piper Approach to SD Car-Following

6 Sizzle Reel Trickery for AI Self-Driving Car Hype

7 Roller Coaster Public Perception of Self-Driving Cars

8 Brainless Self-Driving Shuttles Not Same as SD Cars

9 First Salvo Class Action Lawsuits for Defective SD Cars

10 AI Fake News About Self-Driving Cars

11 Rancorous Ranking of Self-Driving Cars

12 Product Liability for Self-Driving Cars

13 Humans Colliding with Self-Driving Cars

14 Elderly Boon or Bust for Self-Driving Cars

15 Simulations for Self-Driving Cars: Machine Learning

16 DUI Drunk Driving by Self-Driving Cars

17 Ten Human-Driving Foibles: Deep Learning

18 Art of Defensive Driving is Key to Self-Driving Cars

19 Cyclops Approach to AI Self-Driving Cars is Myopic

20 Steering Wheel Gets Self-Driving Car Attention

21 Remote Piloting is a Self-Driving Car Crutch

22 Self-Driving Cars: Zero Fatalities, Zero Chance

23 Goldrush: Self-Driving Car Lawsuit Bonanza Ahead

24 Road Trip Trickery for Self-Driving Trucks and Cars

25 Ethically Ambiguous Self-Driving Car

This title is available via Amazon and other book sellers

Companion Book By This Author

Innovation and Thought Leadership on Self-Driving Driverless Cars

by Dr. Lance B. Eliot, MBA, PhD

Chapter Title

1   Sensor Fusion for Self-Driving Cars

2   Street Scene Free Space Detection Self-Driving Cars

3   Self-Awareness for Self-Driving Cars

4   Cartographic Trade-offs for Self-Driving Cars

5   Toll Road Traversal for Self-Driving Cars

6   Predictive Scenario Modeling for Self-Driving Cars

7   Selfishness for Self-Driving Cars

8   Leap Frog Driving for Self-Driving Cars

9   Proprioceptive IMU's for Self-Driving Cars

10   Robojacking of Self-Driving Cars

11   Self-Driving Car Moonshot and Mother of AI Projects

12   Marketing of Self-Driving Cars

13   Are Airplane Autopilots Same as Self-Driving Cars

14   Savvy Self-Driving Car Regulators: Marc Berman

15   Event Data Recorders (EDR) for Self-Driving Cars

16   Looking Behind You for Self-Driving Cars

17   In-Car Voice Commands NLP for Self-Driving Cars

18   When Self-Driving Cars Get Pulled Over by a Cop

19   Brainjacking Neuroprosthetus Self-Driving Cars

This title is available via Amazon and other book sellers

Companion Book By This Author

New Advances in AI Autonomous Driverless Cars Self-Driving Cars

by Dr. Lance B. Eliot, MBA, PhD

Chapter Title

1 Eliot Framework for AI Self-Driving Cars

2 Self-Driving Cars Learning from Self-Driving Cars

3 Imitation as Deep Learning for Self-Driving Cars

4 Assessing Federal Regulations for Self-Driving Cars

5 Bandwagon Effect for Self-Driving Cars

6 AI Backdoor Security Holes for Self-Driving Cars

7 Debiasing of AI for Self-Driving Cars

8 Algorithmic Transparency for Self-Driving Cars

9 Motorcycle Disentanglement for Self-Driving Cars

10 Graceful Degradation Handling of Self-Driving Cars

11 AI for Home Garage Parking of Self-Driving Cars

12 Motivational AI Irrationality for Self-Driving Cars

13 Curiosity as Cognition for Self-Driving Cars

14 Automotive Recalls of Self-Driving Cars

15 Internationalizing AI for Self-Driving Cars

16 Sleeping as AI Mechanism for Self-Driving Cars

17 Car Insurance Scams and Self-Driving Cars

18 U-Turn Traversal AI for Self-Driving Cars

19 Software Neglect for Self-Driving Cars

This title is available via Amazon and other book sellers

Companion Book By This Author

Introduction to
Driverless Self-Driving Cars

by Dr. Lance B. Eliot, MBA, PhD

Chapter Title

1 Self-Driving Car Moonshot: Mother of All AI Projects
2 Grand Convergence Leads to Self-Driving Cars
3 Why They Should Be Called Self-Driving Cars
4 Richter Scale for Self-Driving Car Levels
5 LIDAR for Self-Driving Cars
6 Overall Framework for Self-Driving Cars
7 Sensor Fusion is Key for Self-Driving Cars
8 Humans Not Fast Enough for Self-Driving Cars
9 Solving Edge Problems of Self-Driving Cars
10 Graceful Degradation for Faltering Self-Driving Cars
11 Genetic Algorithms for Self-Driving Cars
12 Blockchain for Self-Driving Cars
13 Machine Learning and Data for Self-Driving Cars
14 Cyber-Hacking of Self-Driving Cars
15 Sensor Failures in Self-Driving Cars
16 When Accidents Happen to Self-Driving Cars
17 Backdoor Security Holes in Self-Driving Cars
18 Future Brainjacking for Self-Driving Cars
19 Internationalizing Self-Driving Cars
20 Are Airline Autopilots Same as Self-Driving Cars
21 Marketing of Self-Driving Cars
22 Fake News about Self-Driving Cars
23 Product Liability for Self-Driving Cars
24 Zero Fatalities Zero Chance for Self-Driving Cars
25 Road Trip Trickery for Self-Driving Cars
26 Ethical Issues of Self-Driving Cars
27 Ranking of Self-Driving Cars
28 Induced Demand Driven by Self-Driving Cars

This title is available via Amazon and other book sellers

<u>Companion Book By This Author</u>

Autonomous Vehicle Driverless
Self-Driving Cars and Artificial Intelligence

by Dr. Lance B. Eliot, MBA, PhD

<u>Chapter Title</u>

1 Eliot Framework for AI Self-Driving Cars

2 Rocket Man Drivers and AI Self-Driving Cars

3 Occam's Razor Crucial for AI Self-Driving Cars

4 Simultaneous Local/Map (SLAM) for Self-Driving Cars

5 Swarm Intelligence for AI Self-Driving Cars

6 Biomimicry and Robomimicry for Self-Driving Cars

7 Deep Compression/Pruning for AI Self-Driving Cars

8 Extra-Scenery Perception for AI Self-Driving Cars

9 Invasive Curve and AI Self-Driving Cars

10 Normalization of Deviance and AI Self-Driving Cars

11 Groupthink Dilemma for AI Self-Driving Cars

12 Induced Demand Driven by AI Self-Driving Cars

13 Compressive Sensing for AI Self-Driving Cars

14 Neural Layer Explanations for AI Self-Driving Cars

15 Self-Adapting Resiliency for AI Self-Driving Cars

16 Prisoner's Dilemma and AI Self-Driving Cars

17 Turing Test and AI Self-Driving Cars

18 Support Vector Machines for AI Self-Driving Cars

19 "Expert Systems and AI Self-Driving Cars" by Michael Eliot

This title is available via Amazon and other book sellers

Companion Book By This Author
Transformative Artificial Intelligence Driverless Self-Driving Cars

by Dr. Lance B. Eliot, MBA, PhD

Chapter Title

1 Eliot Framework for AI Self-Driving Cars

2 Kinetosis Anti-Motion Sickness for Self-Driving Cars

3 Rain Driving for Self-Driving Cars

4 Edge Computing for Self-Driving Cars

5 Motorcycles as AI Self-Driving Vehicles

6 CAPTCHA Cyber-Hacking and Self-Driving Cars

7 Probabilistic Reasoning for Self-Driving Cars

8 Proving Grounds for Self-Driving Cars

9 Frankenstein and AI Self-Driving Cars

10 Omnipresence for Self-Driving Cars

11 Looking Behind You for Self-Driving Cars

12 Over-The-Air (OTA) Updating for Self-Driving Cars

13 Snow Driving for Self-Driving Cars

14 Human-Aided Training for Self-Driving Cars

15 Privacy for Self-Driving Cars

16 Transduction Vulnerabilities for Self-Driving Cars

17 Conversations Computing and Self-Driving Cars

18 Flying Debris and Self-Driving Cars

19 Citizen AI for Self-Driving Cars

This title is available via Amazon and other book sellers

Companion Book By This Author

Disruptive Artificial Intelligence and Driverless Self-Driving Cars

by Dr. Lance B. Eliot, MBA, PhD

Chapter Title

1   Eliot Framework for AI Self-Driving Cars

2   Maneuverability and Self-Driving Cars

3   Common Sense Reasoning and Self-Driving Cars

4   Cognition Timing and Self-Driving Cars

5   Speed Limits and Self-Driving Vehicles

6   Human Back-up Drivers and Self-Driving Cars

7   Forensic Analysis Uber and Self-Driving Cars

8   Power Consumption and Self-Driving Cars

9   Road Rage and Self-Driving Cars

10 Conspiracy Theories and Self-Driving Cars

11 Fear Landscape and Self-Driving Cars

12 Pre-Mortem and Self-Driving Cars

13 Kits and Self-Driving Cars

This title is available via Amazon and other book sellers

<u>Companion Book By This Author</u>

State-of-the-Art
AI Driverless Self-Driving Cars

by Dr. Lance B. Eliot, MBA, PhD

<u>Chapter Title</u>

1   Eliot Framework for AI Self-Driving Cars

2   Versioning and Self-Driving Cars

3   Towing and Self-Driving Cars

4   Driving Styles and Self-Driving Cars

5   Bicyclists and Self-Driving Vehicles

6   Back-up Cams and Self-Driving Cars

7   Traffic Mix and Self-Driving Cars

8   Hot-Car Deaths and Self-Driving Cars

9   Machine Learning Performance and Self-Driving Cars

10   Sensory Illusions and Self-Driving Cars

11   Federated Machine Learning and Self-Driving Cars

12   Irreproducibility and Self-Driving Cars

13   In-Car Deliveries and Self-Driving Cars

This title is available via Amazon and other book sellers

<u>Companion Book By This Author</u>

Top Trends in
AI Self-Driving Cars

by Dr. Lance B. Eliot, MBA, PhD

<u>Chapter Title</u>

1 Eliot Framework for AI Self-Driving Cars

2 Responsibility and Self-Driving Cars

3 Changing Lanes and Self-Driving Cars

4 Procrastination and Self-Driving Cars

5 NTSB Report and Tesla Car Crash

6 Start Over AI and Self-Driving Cars

7 Freezing Robot Problem and Self-Driving Cars

8 Canarying and Self-Driving Cars

9 Nighttime Driving and Self-Driving Cars

10 Zombie-Cars Taxes and Self-Driving Cars

11 Traffic Lights and Self-Driving Cars

12 Reverse Engineering and Self-Driving Cars

13 Singularity AI and Self-Driving Cars

This title is available via Amazon and other book sellers

Companion Book By This Author

AI Innovations and Self-Driving Cars

by Dr. Lance B. Eliot, MBA, PhD

Chapter Title

1 Eliot Framework for AI Self-Driving Cars

2 API's and Self-Driving Cars

3 Egocentric Designs and Self-Driving Cars

4 Family Road Trip and Self-Driving Cars

5 AI Developer Burnout and Tesla Car Crash

6 Stealing Secrets About Self-Driving Cars

7 Affordability and Self-Driving Cars

8 Crossing the Rubicon and Self-Driving Cars

9 Addicted to Self-Driving Cars

10 Ultrasonic Harm and Self-Driving Cars

11 Accidents Contagion and Self-Driving Cars

12 Non-Stop 24x7 and Self-Driving Cars

13 Human Life Spans and Self-Driving Cars

This title is available via Amazon and other book sellers

Companion Book By This Author

Crucial Advances for
AI Self-Driving Cars

by Dr. Lance B. Eliot, MBA, PhD

Chapter Title

1 Eliot Framework for AI Self-Driving Cars

2 Ensemble Learning and AI Self-Driving Cars

3 Ghost in AI Self-Driving Cars

4 Public Shaming of AI Self-Driving

5 Internet of Things (IoT) and AI Self-Driving Cars

6 Personal Rapid Transit (RPT) and Self-Driving Cars

7 Eventual Consistency and AI Self-Driving Cars

8 Mass Transit Future and AI Self-Driving Cars

9 Coopetition and AI Self-Driving Cars

10 Electric Vehicles (EVs) and AI Self-Driving Cars

11 Dangers of In-Motion AI Self-Driving Cars

12 Sports Cars and AI Self-Driving Cars

13 Game Theory and AI Self-Driving Cars

This title is available via Amazon and other book sellers

<u>Companion Book By This Author</u>

Sociotechnical Insights and AI Driverless Cars

by Dr. Lance B. Eliot, MBA, PhD

<u>Chapter Title</u>

1 Eliot Framework for AI Self-Driving Cars

2 Start-ups and AI Self-Driving Cars

3 Code Obfuscation and AI Self-Driving Cars

4 Hyperlanes and AI Self-Driving Cars

5 Passenger Panic Inside an AI Self-Driving Car

6 Tech Stockholm Syndrome and Self-Driving Cars

7 Paralysis and AI Self-Driving Cars

8 Ugly Zones and AI Self-Driving Cars

9 Ridesharing and AI Self-Driving Cars

10 Multi-Party Privacy and AI Self-Driving Cars

11 Chaff Bugs and AI Self-Driving Cars

12 Social Reciprocity and AI Self-Driving Cars

13 Pet Mode and AI Self-Driving Cars

This title is available via Amazon and other book sellers

Companion Book By This Author

Pioneering Advances for
AI Driverless Cars

by Dr. Lance B. Eliot, MBA, PhD

Chapter Title

1   Eliot Framework for AI Self-Driving Cars

2   Boxes on Wheels and AI Self-Driving Cars

3   Clogs and AI Self-Driving Cars

4   Kids Communicating with AI Self-Driving Cars

5   Incident Awareness and AI Self-Driving Car

6   Emotion Recognition and Self-Driving Cars

7   Rear-End Collisions and AI Self-Driving Cars

8   Autonomous Nervous System and AI Self-Driving Cars

9   Height Warnings and AI Self-Driving Cars

10 Future Jobs and AI Self-Driving Cars

11 Car Wash and AI Self-Driving Cars

12 5G and AI Self-Driving Cars

13 Gen Z and AI Self-Driving Cars

This title is available via Amazon and other book sellers

Companion Book By This Author

Leading Edge Trends for AI Driverless Cars

by Dr. Lance B. Eliot, MBA, PhD

Chapter Title

1   Eliot Framework for AI Self-Driving Cars

2   Pranking and AI Self-Driving Cars

3   Drive-Thrus and AI Self-Driving Cars

4   Overworking on AI Self-Driving Cars

5   Sleeping Barber Problem and AI Self-Driving Cars

6   System Load Balancing and AI Self-Driving Cars

7   Virtual Spike Strips and AI Self-Driving Cars

8   Razzle Dazzle Camouflage and AI Self-Driving Cars

9   Rewilding of AI Self-Driving Cars

10 Brute Force Algorithms and AI Self-Driving Cars

11 Idle Moments and AI Self-Driving Cars

12 Hurricanes and AI Self-Driving Cars

13 Object Visual Transplants and AI Self-Driving Cars

This title is available via Amazon and other book sellers

<u>Companion Book By This Author</u>

The Cutting Edge of AI Autonomous Cars

by Dr. Lance B. Eliot, MBA, PhD

<u>Chapter Title</u>

1 Eliot Framework for AI Self-Driving Cars

2 Driving Controls and AI Self-Driving Cars

3 Bug Bounty and AI Self-Driving Cars

4 Lane Splitting and AI Self-Driving Cars

5 Drunk Drivers versus AI Self-Driving Cars

6 Internal Naysayers and AI Self-Driving Cars

7 Debugging and AI Self-Driving Cars

8 Ethics Review Boards and AI Self-Driving Cars

9 Road Diets and AI Self-Driving Cars

10 Wrong Way Driving and AI Self-Driving Cars

11 World Safety Summit and AI Self-Driving Cars

This title is available via Amazon and other book sellers

Companion Book By This Author

The Next Wave of
AI Self-Driving Cars

by Dr. Lance B. Eliot, MBA, PhD

Chapter Title

1   Eliot Framework for AI Self-Driving Cars

2   Productivity and AI Self-Driving Cars

3   Blind Pedestrians and AI Self-Driving Cars

4   Fail-Safe AI and AI Self-Driving Cars

5   Anomaly Detection and AI Self-Driving Cars

6   Running Out of Gas and AI Self-Driving Cars

7   Deep Personalization and AI Self-Driving Cars

8   Reframing the Levels of AI Self-Driving Cars

9   Cryptojacking and AI Self-Driving Cars

This title is available via Amazon and other book sellers

Revolutionary Innovations of
AI Self-Driving Cars

by Dr. Lance B. Eliot, MBA, PhD

Chapter Title

1 Eliot Framework for AI Self-Driving Cars

2 Exascale Supercomputer and AI Self-Driving Cars

3 Superhuman AI and AI Self-Driving Cars

4 Olfactory e-Nose Sensors and AI Self-Driving Cars

5 Perpetual Computing and AI Self-Driving Cars

6 Byzantine Generals Problem and AI Self-Driving Cars

7 Driver Traffic Guardians and AI Self-Driving Cars

8 Anti-Gridlock Laws and AI Self-Driving Cars

9 Arguing Machines and AI Self-Driving Cars

This title is available via Amazon and other book sellers

Companion Book By This Author

AI Self-Driving Cars
Breakthroughs

by Dr. Lance B. Eliot, MBA, PhD

Chapter Title

1   Eliot Framework for AI Self-Driving Cars

2   Off-Roading and AI Self-Driving Cars

3   Paralleling Vehicles and AI Self-Driving Cars

4   Dementia Drivers and AI Self-Driving Cars

5   Augmented Realty (AR) and AI Self-Driving Cars

6   Sleeping Inside an AI Self-Driving Car

7   Prevalence Detection and AI Self-Driving Cars

8   Super-Intelligent AI and AI Self-Driving Cars

9   Car Caravans and AI Self-Driving Cars

This title is available via Amazon and other book sellers

Companion Book By This Author

Trailblazing Trends for
AI Self-Driving Cars

by Dr. Lance B. Eliot, MBA, PhD

Chapter Title

1 Eliot Framework for AI Self-Driving Cars

2 Strategic AI Metaphors and AI Self-Driving Cars

3 Emergency-Only AI and AI Self-Driving Cars

4 Animal Drawn Vehicles and AI Self-Driving Cars

5 Chess Play and AI Self-Driving Cars

6 Cobots Exoskeletons and AI Self-Driving Car

7 Economic Commodity and AI Self-Driving Cars

8 Road Racing and AI Self-Driving Cars

This title is available via Amazon and other book sellers

Companion Book By This Author

Ingenious Strides for **AI Driverless Cars**

by Dr. Lance B. Eliot, MBA, PhD

Chapter Title

1   Eliot Framework for AI Self-Driving Cars

2   Plasticity and AI Self-Driving Cars

3   NIMBY vs. YIMBY and AI Self-Driving Cars

4   Top Trends for 2019 and AI Self-Driving Cars

5   Rural Areas and AI Self-Driving Cars

6   Self-Imposed Constraints and AI Self-Driving Car

7   Alien Limb Syndrome and AI Self-Driving Cars

8   Jaywalking and AI Self-Driving Cars

This title is available via Amazon and other book sellers

Companion Book By This Author

AI Self-Driving Cars
Inventiveness

by Dr. Lance B. Eliot, MBA, PhD

Chapter Title

1 Eliot Framework for AI Self-Driving Cars

2 Crumbling Infrastructure and AI Self-Driving Cars

3 e-Billboarding and AI Self-Driving Cars

4 Kinship and AI Self-Driving Cars

5 Machine-Child Learning and AI Self-Driving Cars

6 Baby-on-Board and AI Self-Driving Car

7 Cop Car Chases and AI Self-Driving Cars

8 One-Shot Learning and AI Self-Driving Cars

This title is available via Amazon and other book sellers

Companion Book By This Author

Visionary Secrets of AI Driverless Cars

by Dr. Lance B. Eliot, MBA, PhD

Chapter Title

1 Eliot Framework for AI Self-Driving Cars

2 Seat Belts and AI Self-Driving Cars

3 Tiny EV's and AI Self-Driving Cars

4 Empathetic Computing and AI Self-Driving Cars

5 Ethics Global Variations and AI Self-Driving Cars

6 Computational Periscopy and AI Self-Driving Car

7 Superior Cognition and AI Self-Driving Cars

8 Amalgamating ODD's and AI Self-Driving Cars

This title is available via Amazon and other book sellers

Spearheading
AI Self-Driving Cars

by Dr. Lance B. Eliot, MBA, PhD

Chapter Title

1 Eliot Framework for AI Self-Driving Cars

2 Artificial Pain and AI Self-Driving Cars

3 Stop-and-Frisks and AI Self-Driving Cars

4 Cars Careening and AI Self-Driving Cars

5 Sounding Out Car Noises and AI Self-Driving Cars

6 No Speed Limit Autobahn and AI Self-Driving Car

7 Noble Cause Corruption and AI Self-Driving Cars

8 AI Rockstars and AI Self-Driving Cars

This title is available via Amazon and other book sellers

Companion Book By This Author

Spurring
AI Self-Driving Cars

by Dr. Lance B. Eliot, MBA, PhD

Chapter Title

1   Eliot Framework for AI Self-Driving Cars

2   Triune Brain Theory and AI Self-Driving Cars

3   Car Parts Thefts and AI Self-Driving Cars

4   Goto Fail Bug and AI Self-Driving Cars

5   Scrabble Understanding and AI Self-Driving Cars

6   Cognition Disorders and AI Self-Driving Car

7   Noise Pollution Abatement AI Self-Driving Cars

This title is available via Amazon and other book sellers

Companion Book By This Author

Avant-Garde
AI Driverless Cars

by Dr. Lance B. Eliot, MBA, PhD

Chapter Title

1   Eliot Framework for AI Self-Driving Cars

2   Linear Non-Threshold and AI Self-Driving Cars

3   Prediction Equation and AI Self-Driving Cars

4   Modular Autonomous Systems and AI Self-Driving Cars

5   Driver's Licensing and AI Self-Driving Cars

6   Offshoots and Spinoffs and AI Self-Driving Car

7   Depersonalization and AI Self-Driving Cars

This title is available via Amazon and other book sellers

Companion Book By This Author

AI Self-Driving Cars
Evolvement

by Dr. Lance B. Eliot, MBA, PhD

Chapter Title

1   Eliot Framework for AI Self-Driving Cars

2   Chief Safety Officers and AI Self-Driving Cars

3   Bounded Volumes and AI Self-Driving Cars

4   Micro-Movements Behaviors and AI Self-Driving Cars

5   Boeing 737 Aspects and AI Self-Driving Cars

6   Car Controls Commands and AI Self-Driving Car

7   Multi-Sensor Data Fusion and AI Self-Driving Cars

This title is available via Amazon and other book sellers

<u>Companion Book By This Author</u>

AI Driverless Cars
Chrysalis

by Dr. Lance B. Eliot, MBA, PhD

<u>Chapter Title</u>

1 Eliot Framework for AI Self-Driving Cars

2 Object Poses and AI Self-Driving Cars

3 Human In-The-Loop and AI Self-Driving Cars

4 Genius Shortage and AI Self-Driving Cars

5 Salvage Yards and AI Self-Driving Cars

6 Precision Scheduling and AI Self-Driving Car

7 Human Driving Extinction and AI Self-Driving Cars

This title is available via Amazon and other book sellers

Companion Book By This Author

Boosting
AI Autonomous Cars

by Dr. Lance B. Eliot, MBA, PhD

Chapter Title

1 Eliot Framework for AI Self-Driving Cars

2 Zero Knowledge Proofs and AI Self-Driving Cars

3 Active Shooter Response and AI Self-Driving Cars

4 Free Will and AI Self-Driving Cars

5 No Picture Yet of AI Self-Driving Cars

6 Boeing 737 Lessons and AI Self-Driving Cars

7 Preview Tesla FSD and AI Self-Driving Cars

8 LIDAR Industry and AI Self-Driving Cars

9 Uber IPO and AI Self-Driving Cars

10 Suing Automakers of AI Self-Driving Cars

11 Tesla Overarching FSD and AI Self-Driving Cars

12 Auto Repair Market and AI Self-Driving Cars

This title is available via Amazon and other book sellers

ABOUT THE AUTHOR

Dr. Lance B. Eliot, MBA, PhD is the CEO of Techbruim, Inc. and Executive Director of the Cybernetic AI Self-Driving Car Institute, and has over twenty years of industry experience including serving as a corporate officer in a billion dollar firm and was a partner in a major executive services firm. He is also a serial entrepreneur having founded, ran, and sold several high-tech related businesses. He previously hosted the popular radio show *Technotrends* that was also available on American Airlines flights via their in-flight audio program. Author or co-author of a dozen books and over 400 articles, he has made appearances on CNN, and has been a frequent speaker at industry conferences.

A former professor at the University of Southern California (USC), he founded and led an innovative research lab on Artificial Intelligence in Business. Known as the "AI Insider" his writings on AI advances and trends has been widely read and cited. He also previously served on the faculty of the University of California Los Angeles (UCLA), and was a visiting professor at other major universities. He was elected to the International Board of the Society for Information Management (SIM), a prestigious association of over 3,000 high-tech executives worldwide.

He has performed extensive community service, including serving as Senior Science Adviser to the Vice Chair of the Congressional Committee on Science & Technology. He has served on the Board of the OC Science & Engineering Fair (OCSEF), where he is also has been a Grand Sweepstakes judge, and likewise served as a judge for the Intel International SEF (ISEF). He served as the Vice Chair of the Association for Computing Machinery (ACM) Chapter, a prestigious association of computer scientists. Dr. Eliot has been a shark tank judge for the USC Mark Stevens Center for Innovation on start-up pitch competitions, and served as a mentor for several incubators and accelerators in Silicon Valley and Silicon Beach. He served on several Boards and Committees at USC, including having served on the Marshall Alumni Association (MAA) Board in Southern California.

Dr. Eliot holds a PhD from USC, MBA, and Bachelor's in Computer Science, and earned the CDP, CCP, CSP, CDE, and CISA certifications. Born and raised in Southern California, and having traveled and lived internationally, he enjoys scuba diving, surfing, and sailing.

ADDENDUM

Boosting
AI Autonomous Cars

Practical Advances in Artificial Intelligence (AI)
and Machine Learning

By

Dr. Lance B. Eliot, MBA, PhD

———

For supplemental materials of this book, visit:

www.ai-selfdriving-cars.guru

For special orders of this book, contact:

LBE Press Publishing

Email: LBE.Press.Publishing@gmail.com